God's finger on
My Bedroom wall

Could this be an End-time Strategy?

Dr. Nicku Kyungu Mordi

Author's Contact information:

Dr. Nicku Kyungu Mordi
President
I GO Africa for Jesus Prayer Movement, Inc. &
Africa Transformation Embassy, Inc.

P.O. Box 698
Beltsville, MD 20705

Email: igoministries@gmail.com or
director@atembassy.org
www.igoafricaforjesus.org;
www.atembassy.org
+1 301 580 3645

Cover and Layout by:
Bidea Communications Limited

TABLE OF CONTENTS

ACKNOWLEDGEMENT

It is impossible to acknowledge all who have played different roles in this movement. However, it would be impossible to share this end-time strategy if the churches listed below did not heed God's call to unite and claim Africa and America for Jesus. I thank God for their willingness to unite as the Body of Christ in the Washington Metropolitan area and beyond. Thank you for all you have done to impact nations around the world, you supported God's mandate from 1993 and God's revelation will manifest as you continue to build end-time unity to decree and declare thanksgiving for nations. Thank YOU!

- Bethel World Outreach Church in Silver Spring, Maryland
- The Redeemed Christian Church of God - Jesus House, Washington D.C.
- Christ Apostolic Church of America, Hyattsville, Maryland
- Christ Gospel Church, Silver Spring, Maryland
- Church of the Living God, Hyattsville, Maryland
- Ethiopian Int'l Evangelical Church, Washington, D.C.

- Action Faith Ministries, Washington, D.C.
- Faith & Victory Christian Center, Alexandria, Virginia
- Oracles of God's Mission Church, Lanham, Maryland
- The Redeemed Christian Chureh of God - Victory Temple, Bowie, Maryland
- Refuge of Hope Disciple Center, Washington, D.C.
- End-Time Glory Center International, Alexandria, Virginia
- Christian Victory Center, Takoma Park, Maryland
- Discipleship Ministries International, District Heights, Maryland
- Open Bible International Church, Alexandria, Virginia
- Bright Light Baptist Church, Takoma Park, Maryland
- Africa Methodist Episcopal Church, Baltimore, Maryland
- Power Christian Ministry Int'l Center, Langley Park, Maryland

NOTE: THE SENIOR PASTORS PLAYED DIFFERENT LEADERSHIP ROLES FOR HIS GLORY!

INTRODUCTION

T he Wisest man that lived said, "There *is a time for everything, and a season for every activity under heaven."* He continued by saying, *"...there is nothing better for men than to be happy and do good while they live"* (Eccles. 3:1,12). In that context I believe the pattern God divinely wrote and mandated the Body of Christ to adopt for end-time purpose was a reminder to His Children of who they are. He wrote dates on my bedroom wall from 1994-2006, a 12-year span. Several times since then, He has spoken concerning this Third Saturday mandate to unite the Body of Christ for end-time impact and to continue to demonstrate His Word. "If we are one, then the world would believe in Jesus".

There is an undeniable fact that some people do not understand why the Church exists today. In other words, if the purpose of the Body of Christ is understood, then walking and working in unity would be easy and a priority! The mystery of God writing dates on my bedroom wall and giving instructions for Christians to unite cannot be understood but must be obeyed. This mandate to unite once a month to pray started 26 years ago and since that time, several supernatural evidences have enforced the Third Saturday Prayer Unity mandate. There is a sense of understanding as to why God is keen to see His children walk and live in unity while at the same time appreciating their diversity. Therefore, in this book, I attempt to reveal what we have discovered or learned in accordance with the Word of God. Some of the reasons as to why God wrote those dates to reflect the Biblical reference to the Third Day phenomena will become clear in the chapters ahead.

God never intended for His people to all be the same. He created each one of us differently and gave us unique talents, visions and dreams; however, He expects us to use our God-given abilities and talents to fulfill one purpose; that is, to be His Ambassadors on planet earth to fulfill His Kingdom agenda. Unity is exhibited in different ways; for instance, belonging to the same denomination or church, being part of the same ministry or being from the same nation. God's mandate of unity among His children must bring all these different visions, dreams, denominations, professions and systems together; to have the same knowledge that Christ has united us for the sole purpose of bringing His Kingdom to earth. This strategy requires us to pray together giving thanks, praise and to make decrees on communities and nations for God's Kingdom to come. For His kingdom agenda to be realized, we must make a concerted effort to walk in one accord as we see in John 17:21-23 when Jesus prayed,

> *"That all of them may be one, Father, just as you are in me and I am in you. May they also be in us so that the world may believe that you have sent me. I have given them the glory that you gave me, that they may be one as we are one. I in them and you in me. May they be brought to complete unity to let the world know that you sent me and have loved them even as you have loved me."*

This book is about sharing what God revealed with evidence that others could see, as well as how He spoke to some other people about what He showed me. As you read this book therefore, be open to the guidance of the Holy Spirit. Desire to be God's conduit for expressing His love towards uniting His Body to be light and salt. I am confident that since the entire movement of the Third Saturday Unity was initiated by God, He would reveal the action to take in line with what He wrote.

More so, I believe that, whoever you are, you will strive to unite in your own communities once a month — not to pray for your own needs but that of your community and nation according to the strategy God has revealed.

As you pray and make declarations, rely completely on the authority of the scriptures to bring His Kingdom on earth for His honor and glory alone. Also, you must put into account how Moses, when he was about to build a tabernacle, was told to follow everything according to the pattern he was shown by God (Hebrews 8:5b). This end-time unity of impact, must be followed exactly how God showed it to be done; that is according to the specific dates God wrote on my bedroom wall. It would amaze you, how those who never wanted to associate with you or church, those who despised Christianity would start to be attracted to follow Christ.

CHAPTER ONE

UNITY TO ACCOMPLISH THE GREAT COMMISSION

C hristian unity is important in our individual lives and it is important in our churches to make disciples of all nations. Each child of God is in unity with the Father and the Son as we read in the Gospel of John 17:21., "...*that all of them may be one, Father, just as you are in me and I am in you.*" Moreover, this unity demands that we work in love as Christ — who is in us — loves us, John 15:9-17 says,

> "*As the Father has loved me, so have I loved you. Now remain in my love. If you obey my commandment, you will remain in my love, just as I have obeyed my Father's commandments and remain in his love. I have told you this so that my joy may be in you......you did*

not choose me, but I chose you to go ad bear fruit- fruit that will last., Then the Father will give you whatever you ask in my name. This is my command, Love each other"

We must get this revelation that Christ's love is in us – He is the one who will help us to love one another and to walk in the unity that has already been accomplished. It is through that divine revelatory knowledge of Christ that gives us understanding of all the things that have been provided for us. Knowing this reality will cause you to live in abundant peace, grace and to avoid evil desires that create division. We cannot accomplish the unity mandate without Christ's love dwelling in us richly. But when we sincerely depend on Him and are willing to be led by the Holy Spirit, we are able to do all things, such as walking in unity and loving each other.

Disunity is Not Good Witness

Apostle Paul had so much to say about unity. He agreed that we are many, but one body through Jesus Christ. Then another time he said we should all speak the same thing (Rom. 12:5; 1 Cor. 1:10). These scriptures indicate that we can be united in our diversity. If Christians are not walking in the unity that Christ provided, "then the world would not believe" (John 17:21). If unbelievers see Christians fighting among themselves or demeaning other churches because they are different or are not of their denominations nor affiliations, they would not attract those who are unbelievers and that is not a good witness to our Lord as well as to the society we are trying to win for Christ. In order to be Salt and Light, we should endeavor to speak as Paul advised the Philippians believers in Philippians 4:8

"Whatever is true, whatever is noble, whatever is right, whatever if pure, whatever is lovely, whatever if admirable, if anything is excellent or praiseworthy – think about such things."

Peter also wrote that we ought to love one another with a pure heart fervently as recorded in 1 Peter 1:22.

"Now that you have purified yourselves by obeying the truth so that you have sincere love for your brothers, love one another deeply, from the heart."

Indeed, Christians are people who belong to different churches, they belong to various denominations, but they all belong to One God, He is the master planner of our diversity. I thank God we are all different, different nationalities, different sizes and different shades of our skin. When you travel, you see different natural sceneries that demonstrate God's power of creativity. Diversity makes the world beautiful and pleases the Creator. Yet in our diversity, God commands us to love and appreciate one another which is the perfect bond of unity and peace.

Diversity in the Body is Strength

As mentioned above, the Word of God shows Christian unity is the heart of God. Before the foundation of the earth God loved each of us individually and He commanded us to love one another as Christ loved the church. Discord and division are unnatural for the children of God. Our diversity should make the body stronger because each person has a specific assignment, talent or vision to accomplish the Great Commission. When love, respect, and appreciation for one another is expressed, and when we esteem one another more highly than ourselves, it glorifies God, the Bible says;

> *"Therefore if you have any encouragement from being united with Christ, if any comfort from his love, if any common sharing in the Spirit, if any tenderness and compassion, then make my joy complete by being like-minded, having the same love, being one in spirit and of one mind. Do nothing out of selfish ambition or vain conceit. Rather, in humility value others above yourselves, not looking to your own interests but each of you to the interests of the others. In your relationships with one another, have the same mindset as Christ Jesus" (Philippians 2:1-5)*

This emphasis on unity in scripture, is in line with the mandate of the Third Saturday unity will be expounded to the last detail in the subsequent chapters. It is a reminder for God's children to follow for end-time impact. It is a simple strategy, but not yet understood. It simply means Christians in their churches, in their denominations, ministries and businesses, on the third Saturday of a month are to agree and gather to speak and declare the same things. They would all, in one accord, pray for their communities, societies or nations to experience and enjoy the benefits of Kingdom living.

On the third Saturday, Christians are to unite not to pray for their personal or church needs but that of their communities and nations. They are to meet to thank God for all He does, the many prayers He has answered and the ones He will answer. Together as a community, Christians are to speak or declare His will to be established in the areas that are of concern to your society and nation. You are also to unite to seek the mind of God on how to solve any problem that is in your communities, society or nation. When unchurched people realize what Christians are doing for their communities, the Body of Christ would become relevant in that location and gain influence. Anywhere Christians strive to touch people, regardless of their faith or skin color, there is transformation in that community, society and nation.

Misconception of the Great Commission

Apart from the misunderstanding many believers have as to why the Church exists, the command of the Great Commission (go into all the world) is also misunderstood.

Many interpret it to be going to another country or traveling to a geographical location. In Greek, the word WORLD means cosmos, 'systems' of power, system order — the entire universe, 'all God's creations' are to be reached with the love of God. We must go into all the *systems of power in every society* and teach what Jesus taught. People in these systems must become students of what we believe as Christians; we are to teach all nations to be students, pupils or apprentices of Jesus.

God has created different systems and the followers of Christ must be able to teach the doctrines of scripture and the lifestyle of the kingdom of God in every system of power. Followers of Christ should help governing systems not to violate any natural law that God put in place during creation nor the divine law written in Scriptures. He is the Creator of everything and He has put guiding laws in place. It is our responsibility to disciple or teach nations to observe these laws in order to live in peace and harmony — it is not the work of politicians to disciple nations; it is the work of Christ's loving people. Proverbs 14:34 says, *"Righteousness exalts a nation, but sin is a disgrace to any people."* Righteousness is found only in Jesus Christ who commanded us to GO into all the world and make disciples.

When you consider the larger Body of Christ, the many people that are not being discipled in the churches today, then you would understand why the Great Commission is not yet understood fully. Jesus taught His followers, who became His disciples. In other words, Jesus was their teacher. After they were taught, He commissioned them to go into every system to be teachers. These days however, some church leaders and pastors, especially in the non-denominational churches, have not understood the importance of discipleship. They start churches based on miracles or anointing alone without the emphasis of knowing the scriptures. This is one of the reasons why there are many divisions and false teachers who continue to preach wrong doctrine.

Years of Ungodly Practice in Churches

Unfortunately, for the last century, we have become more divided than ever before. Some congregations are divided over minor things like color of the carpet or church furniture. Some are divided because of the songs they want to be sung during the services; some because of the issue of finances. Then there are those who are divided because of doctrinal issues which is the cause of the various denominations. Since the 20th century, the division in Pentecostal churches have escalated because everyone wants to be in charge; some use all kinds of gimmicks to enrich themselves — peoples' ego is causing the Body of Christ to suffer and the Kingdom mandate is being accomplished at a very slow pace.

I recall how God showed the disunity that existed during the 2012 Mandate Africa tour to Israel. The last day of the tour, the leadership team prepared seven doves that were held by seven Mandate Africa leaders from South Africa. As they released the doves to indicate "Mission accomplished," five doves flew away but two of them remained under the podium. Several people tried to make them fly, but the doves refused to fly. They remained on the podium till the entire program was finished. It was a strange sight and no one could explain why the two doves refused to fly. The program ended and we left, leaving the doves on the podium.

Around 3 a.m. the following morning, I was awakened by a familiar voice that prompted me to look out. As I rubbed my eyes to see clearly, I saw two doves outside my hotel widow. One held a Christian Unity Flag that said, "Praying for Africa" and another one was holding a sign written "WORD." In my disbelieve and shock, I walked towards the window and tried to make them fly away, but they didn't. Then God told me clearly what He wanted me to do and why five doves flew away and two didn't. In summary He said, "Number two represents unity but there was no unity among the leadership team and they refused to do what they were instructed to do." He continued to say, "They fulfilled their agenda but not My mandate, and that is why I could not let the doves fly. However, My grace is still upon the church to fulfill My kingdom agenda; that is why five of the doves flew away." Indeed, five is a number of grace and some Churches are not consumed because of His grace. That night when God spoke, it was a frightening encounter. The thought of it brings me to my knees and I do not get tired of reminding His Body of our need to obey His mandate and walk in unity to fulfill the Kingdom agenda.

Unity is Part of His death

The death of Jesus Christ 2000 years ago is supposed to unite us as one Body, but in reality, we do not act as ONE! Even those who believe the same doctrine and worship in the same church are still divided because of one thing or another, and some are divided because of reasons earlier mentioned. Apostle Paul, through God's Word encouraged Christians in their own denominations, ministries, churches, and in their God-given visions to walk and work in unity (Hebrew 12:2-3). This is because each vision, each ministry that came from God is to accomplish a bigger purpose; one which is far more important than any of us can comprehend. We need to celebrate the different talents and ministries; each is for the purpose of fulfilling the Great Commission if we follow God's design and pattern. The Word of God in the epistle to the Philippians 4:11-13 says,

"It is Him who gave some to be apostles, some to be prophets, some to be evangelists, and some to be pastors

and teachers to prepare God's people for works of service so that the body of Christ may be built up..."

No one ministry, church or denomination can accomplish God's plan for planet earth. In whatever we are called to do, the Word of God must be our yardstick. This is the time and season to make every effort to unite to prepare God's people for Kingdom service as we recognize their uniqueness and giftings. In the Old Testament, God was specific to give assignment with instructions on patterns to follow. For instance, Moses, the deliverer of God's people, was also given specific instructions for something as small as a lampstand (Numbers 8:3-4). For some people, God's giftings to advance His Kingdom comes with instructions that must be obeyed to benefit His Body. Hebrews 8:5b reminds us of how Moses was warned when he was about to build the tabernacle: *"See to it that you make everything according to the PATTERN shown you on the mountain."* This book is also about a pattern for the Body of Christ to follow — the strategy God revealed on the bedroom wall. God's Third Saturday requirement for intentional unity to advance His Kingdom has a biblical interpretation.

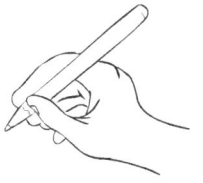

CHAPTER TWO

PATTERNS IN GOD'S WORD

W hen reading the Word of God, we must always remember God's Word is alive and He designed His Word with purposeful patterns and symmetry that prove that He inspired it. We can see God's designs and patterns not only through types and parallels, but also in numbers and in the meaning of names of people and places. God always speaks through His Word and according to His Word. His purpose and plans must be accomplished in our individual lives for His Kingdom to be manifested on the earth through His Word and His methods or strategies the Holy Spirit gives.

"The Word of God is living and active, sharper than any doubled-edged sword. It penetrates even to dividing soul and spirit, joints and marrow;

it judges the thoughts and attitudes of the heart"
(Hebrews 4:12).

Indeed, there is nothing like the Word of God! If we truly understood what this means, we would love and honor the Word. We would be conscious of the Holy Spirit's presence in our lives. I am thankful for all the teachers of the Word of God and every book that has been written to teach us on how to study His Word. There is nothing as important and rewarding as reading the Word of God daily. The Word is alive and active to help you and guide you in any situation that you are facing or that you might face in the future.

God's Word is Divine

Furthermore, in this book, I want us to study the patterns or the importance of **the Number 3** in the Bible. In the beginning, God set the pattern of the days of the weeks. From God's perspective, a day is a thousand years: *For a thousand years in Your sight are like yesterday when it is past, and like a watch in the night, (Psalm 90:4).* In another scripture, Peter tells us not to be ignorant! He said, *"But, beloved, do not forget this one thing, that with the Lord one day is as a thousand years, and a thousand years as one day"* (2 Peter 3:8).

I am trying to establish a premise that we cannot try to understand God's Word like we understand or study any other subject on planet earth. God speaks things that are beyond the natural understanding that many try to reason through to understand using their five senses. By doing so many have missed God's leading for them, their families and their nations. We must understand spiritual things using our spirit within us. Then we would see, "deep things of God." The Bible says,

> *"But we speak the wisdom of God in a mystery, the hidden wisdom which God ordained before the ages for our glory, which none of the rulers of this age knew …. as it is written: "Eye has not seen, nor ear heard, nor have entered into the heart of man the things which God has prepared for those who love Him." But God has revealed them to us through His Spirit. For the Spirit searches all things, yes, the deep things of God". (1 Corinthians 2:7-10)*

God's Timely Agenda for His people

In my first book: *Blind Faith: God's Amazing Miracles,* I wrote on how God speaks to me and how my life's journey has been obeisance to things that don't make sense. A life of listening and obeying God by taking action even if I didn't understand has never been boring. It is filled with excitement, anticipation and anticipation of the unknown. I know in this dispensation God wants to accomplish so much beyond what any of us have ever experienced before. The Holy Spirit is about to finish the book of Acts using sincere Apostles of today who are ordinary Christians filled with zeal to advance God's Kingdom.

During the birth of the Church in the First century, the Holy Spirit worked through ordinary people, showing them where to go, whom to contact and even how to speak to the rulers. Luke, the author of the Book of Acts in the New Testament, finished the Book of Acts with Chapter 28 leaving Paul in prison in Rome to preach and teach about the Lord Jesus Christ. 'Chapter 29' and onwards are being written by the lives of the many unsung heroes who have continued and are changing the world with the changeless message of God's love and His grace, at least for those who are willing to accept Jesus as their Lord and Savior.

This is what we must continue to do: preach the Gospel using every strategy the Holy Spirit gives to us. We have a great tool with the advancement of technology; if used wisely, we can advance God's Kingdom in every sphere of life. As we continue this study, it is important to note that parallels and patterns should never be used to form new doctrines, but rather as a support to what has already been revealed by the Holy Spirit through the clear teaching of the Word of God.

Awesome Presence of God

There are many things God does in various parts of the world with different people which are not known to the rest of the Body of Christ. Thank God today's internet is helping to reveal what goes on in other parts of the world. In this book, I am trying to reveal some simple strategies God exposed by writing down numbers on my bedroom wall.

The fact that He took time to write them down rather than dictate to me, has given me a very strong desire to seek the awesome presence of God in my life. He knew what He was giving was important and divine. He did not want me to get confused or to mess up. Moreover, He knew I could not retain all the numbers in the 12 years' span. He had to come down to my room to write the instructions and told me to copy what He had written. I did not have to calculate or figure out what it meant; I did not even have to question why He was 'messing up' my white wall with ink nor ask why me? What I did was obey and accept what He told me to do. I didn't even ask if what He was doing was in accordance to scripture — He Himself is the WORD and His presence was too awesome for me to say anything!

I often tell people, if you receive any revelation or vision that contradicts the Word of God, you have to dismiss it. God always speaks through His Word and according to

His Word. That night, I did not dare to question Him; I sat there in shock and numb — I could not think. All I could do was follow His instruction to copy the numbers He had written. What God revealed in 1994 is what expound in this book with the hope that the entire Christendom would take on this simple end-time strategy to fulfill the Great Commission.

The strategy He revealed does not require anyone to change what God has called them to do. It does not require anyone to remove anything from their church or change anything in their ministry operation; rather, God wants to enhance and promote whatever you are doing. He wants to improve your situation and take you to a higher level of influence than ever before.

Listen and Hear — God Speaks

In 1993, God said He had heard the prayers of His people. When He spoke those words, it reminded me of the 1979 event when He instructed me not to get the train ticket to go to preach with Moses Kulola (the biggest evangelist in Tanzania at the time) in Mwanza, but instead get a ticket to go to Kitwe, Zambia. It was so strange because Zambia was not in my plans nor did I pray to go there on that particular trip. I had just finished preaching at an open-air crusade at the Uhuru ground organized by the Ilala Assemblies of God Church in Dar es Salaam, Tanzania — God did great miracles, many people got saved, the deaf and dumb were healed and many were delivered. After the crusade, two young men who were guest singers approached and invited me to go to preach in their country. I really did not pay any attention to what they were saying because I was tired and knew it was impossible. My last crusade before I returned to Sweden was arranged to be in the West Region of Tanzania. I was young then and zealous to go minister with a very famous Assemblies of God National Evangelist, so I could not entertain another invitation to any other country. However, God had a different plan for me.

When He spoke and stopped me at that train station, I had to obey and change my plans to His plans — just like in the Old Testament when God interrupted Moses' plan and sent him to deliver His people from bondage in Egypt. God told Moses He had heard and seen the cry of His children in Egypt

"And now the cry of the Israelites has reached me, and I have seen the way the Egyptians are oppressing them. ¹⁰ So now, go. I am sending you to Pharaoh to bring my people the Israelites out of Egypt." *(Exodus 3:9-10).*

God does not want anyone to perish; all must hear and experience His love for all generations. He is the same God that still speaks today. Around the world, there are evidences of different intercessory prayers that are being answered. God hears the prayers of His people and He hears your prayers. He sends evidence or a word with someone to encourage you that He is not dead. God desires and wants you as His child to know that you are being heard. Many times, He has answered your prayers. However, sometimes the manifestation does not come because: a) the timing is not right; b) we are not ready to handle what His answer might be. c) we are praying amiss.

There is also another factor that some of us don't consider. Your prayers have been answered but (a) you are really not expecting to receive the answers. (b) you have not positioned yourself to receive. (c) you have left the place or position where the answer or gift was to be delivered.

For example, if Elijah had left the Brook of Cherith where God commanded the Ravens to deliver lunch and dinner to him (1 Kings 17:2-4), no amount of prayer would have delivered his meals to his new location. Some of you who have waited for the manifestation of your prayers would be shocked to see shelves filled with your gifts that you thought God did not answer. And it would be your fault for changing your location — a place called "There." This location is sometimes your mind, you stopped believing for what you prayed for. Or you changed location by confessing negativity. What you say or speak can nullify your prayers. Sometimes you do not receive because you give up too soon or for the many other reasons.

Divine Strategy of Same-Day Prayers

This book is to enhance end-time Christian Unity to expand God's Kingdom in every sphere of society using the Third Saturday divine strategy and mandate to fulfill the great commission in every sphere of life. There is no doubt prayer is common to all, strategic prayer is the only key to invoke unity that will last. Every Christian, every church and every ministry, regardless of denominational or doctrinal preference, can participate. It does not matter how the prayers are made as long as they are biblically inspired and in the name of the Lord Jesus Christ.

Christians, to enforce the unity mandate, are to once in a month unite to offer relational kind of prayers of thanksgiving to God. It is a gathering to give God honor, praise and thanksgiving in prayer. It is for all who have confidence with God as their Father and acknowledge that they are God's children who pray according to His will to expect and see results. They know they have the authority to decree a thing and it would be established (Job 22:26-30) [Read my book, Never Forgotten: Advice for all God's children]. The book gives evidences of how supernatural miracles took place by word of mouth.

In my 54 years of walking with God and serving others for His glory, I have seen people who pray effectively and the others who only read prayers that were written for them which they do as a routine or as an assignment to fulfill. Prayer is the fuel of our existence; prayer is the oxygen in our spiritual lungs; it is not a ministry but a lifestyle. People with this understanding and practice experience victorious living in spite of the problems and challenges they may face. They understand that nothing would be able to separate them from the Love of Christ

> *Who shall separate us from the love of Christ? Shall trouble or hardship or persecution or famine or nakedness or danger or sword. No, in all these things we are more than conquerors through him who loved us. For I am convinced that neither death nor life, neither angels nor demons, neither the present nor the future, nor any powers, neither height nor depth, nor anything else in all creation, will be able to separate us from the love of God that is in Christ Jesus our Lord,"* (Romans 8:35-39).

These people who have a lifestyle of prayer have different priorities; they understand that Jesus himself accomplished His mission on earth because of the lifestyle of prayer. They also remember the saying of Jesus when He said, *"man always ought to pray"* (Luke 18:1; 21:36).

The Apostle Paul echoed what Jesus said by encouraging Christians in Thessalonica to *pray without ceasing* (I Thess. 5:17); He continued by saying, *"pray with all kind of prayers"* (Ephesians 6:16). When you live a lifestyle of prayer, you are without fear because you are totally secure in God. God's divine favor would be the norm in your life and experiencing supernatural miracles would be a frequent occurrence as well.

CHAPTER THREE

GOD IN MY BEDROOM

Christians all over the world understand the importance of prayer and they are praying all the time. Many have testimonies of how God used them to transform communities, cities, and nations through prayer — To God be all the glory. This is why He wants their prayers to make greater impact than it currently does. God wants to do much more than what we have seen. I know firsthand, my lifestyle of engaging God in intimate prayer is the source of my energy and zeal to serve Him for all these years.

My life is filled with the supernatural because often my prayers are without speaking so many words; I let my spirit, soul and body to be locked in deep communion with God. This can be very intimate and those around might not detect anything, often they assume negatively because I am not noisy. Indeed, there is a time for every activity — a time to pray out loud and a time to pray silently.

In one of these times, I had a visitation in my room. God told me to add to my prayer life another strategy that would benefit the Body of Christ. In His own divine will He showed me a strategy that I had never thought about or asked Him about. Up until now, I marvel that God Himself saw fit to elevate me to another level in my spiritual journey. *"But solid food is for the mature, who by constant use have trained themselves to distinguish good from evil"* (Hebrews 5:14). It is awesome to think that God came down to my room to give me a strategy for His people. He spoke to me but not for me alone.

On that day, He told me to disseminate the instruction to all leaders of the Christian faith in the Washington Metropolitan area and everywhere else in order to unite for the redemption of all people for God's kingdom to come on earth as it is in heaven

Refusing to Hear God Speak

Before that visitation in my bedroom, God had spoken vividly about how unity would be enhanced among African leaders and their people. Although I heard it, I did not understand; it did not make sense. So, I ignored it and continued my usual rounds in the church and community. I really did not want to be bothered with anything different — I was tired of being the one doing what was uncommon or unpopular. I didn't express any enthusiasm to understand what He told me, but I could not shake off the conviction I felt in my spirit. I had a sense that God was trying to say something in my spirit, but I continued to ignore the feeling and pretended it was not Him.

Three months passed then I heard a ring in my ears followed by an urgent audible voice that said to listen and obey. It reminded me of the voice of God I heard in 1977 when He told me audibly to resign from my best job with the American Embassy in Dar es Salaam, Tanzania to go and be a missionary/evangelist in Sweden. I did not want to hear that nor to believe it was God speaking. "How could a young African girl be told to go to Northern Europe by an invisible being?" That sounded crazy and I did not want to hear it. However, as I surrendered to obey without any assurance of anything, the Holy Spirit started showing me what to do one step at a time. I yielded and said, "Not my will Lord, but your will be done."

What I am writing about is hard to explain unless you have experienced Godly visitations. Unless you have had an encounter with God on a personal level, there are things or experiences you would easily dismiss as impossible, but because I live it, I want you, who is reading, to understand that God is real and He still speaks. My entire Christian journey is a life lived by trusting the Word and depending on the Holy Spirit's leading. By faith, I have travelled to 50 nations because God speaks and directs me on where to go and what to do.

This life does not, however, get any easier, I am still learning after all these years. When He speaks, I do not always obey immediately. I argue, refuse or ignore, I cannot say I am used to how He speaks, no! Every experience is different. Especially when what He says does not make sense to me — which is often the case. Now you can understand why it does not make sense to those who hear it. They would think I have lost my mind and say all manner of things when I am not around. At times my own children say, "Mom, you are delusional" or as my husband would say, "You are out of touch with the real world."

Indeed, if anyone hesitates to believe what is revealed, I do not blame them. It is hard to accept things that are spiritually revealed and are not the norm. With time, I have become a little better in acting by faith without understanding exactly what God is saying. To this day, I sometimes do not always immediately obey. I admire and give God all the honor for His longsuffering with me. Although I don't say "Yes" immediately, He does not give up or stop speaking, He is patient and I honor Him for not giving up on me.

As He continued to talk about uniting all Christians in the Washington Metro area in November 1993, I had to obey and take a step of faith, look for a location and start inviting Christian leaders from different churches and denominations to unite with this specific appeal: "Are you concerned about your community? Are you concerned about your nation? Do you want God to intervene in your situation? Then come so we can unite as one to claim Africa for Jesus, I used II Chronicles 7:14 as our mobilizing scripture,

> *"If my people, who are called by my name, will humble themselves and pray and seek my face and turn from their wicked ways, then I will hear from heaven, and I will forgive their sin and will heal their land."*

In those days, what God was asking me to do was an impossible task. In the DC Metro area, many churches focused on gathering people from their original countries and some according to their own ethnic groups. Others got together because they were from the same denominational background. It was a noble thing to connect with people with whom you share culture, ethnicity even denominational affiliations. Now imagine trying to tell them to unite as Christians who are concerned about praying for Africa and other nations. People were into praying for their own countries, their own needs and seeking God to intervene in their situation in a foreign land. To ask them to be concerned with other nations in the Continent was something unheard of at that time. People were happy to fellowship according to their own kind and pray for their own families and friends both here and abroad.

Enduring the Scorn

When they heard what I was told to do, many discouraged me, especially since I was not heading any congregation in a church setting but only a volunteer associate minister of a church which was known as The Ghanaian church. Some even ridiculed me, "Who do you think you are? You are new to the Washington Metropolitan Area; you cannot succeed in bringing different church leaders from different countries and denominations together? Don't you see! Even people from the same country are divided because they are from different tribes. My dear, tribalism is not in Africa alone but even in America!" I heard so many voices telling me how impossible it was and there were voices within me that affirmed what they were saying and in my mind, I thought, "Definitely this will not work!"

Hearing negativity from the people I love, even from my own thoughts at times, could have caused me to disobey

God. However, one element that gave me courage was the reality that I had nothing to do with the idea! To pray and claim nations for Jesus by uniting people from different nations did not come from me. On my own, I could not have even thought of such a brilliant idea or strategy to unify His Body in our area. I was too busy speaking as well as doing visitations to church members or travelling on missions and doing several humanitarian projects in the villages of Africa to engage in another program. It was easy to dismiss the instruction and accept that it was impossible. But because God kept on speaking, I accepted the reality that God had spoken to me. The more they opposed and told me of how impossible the task was, the more I realized it was a Godly assignment and took different steps to plan for the service: looking for a space, deciding on the time of the meeting and then making a flyer to promote the prayers for nations and declare "Africa for Jesus."

I searched the names of every African country and their presidents or heads of States in order to call them by name as we prayed — This was part of the instruction God gave, "Call the name of each county and president, including the United States of America and her president." Imagine, in 1993, there was no internet, finding the names of every country and their presidents was not easy. Nevertheless, because I knew I had heard from God, by faith I kept on planning with confidence and encouraging myself through His Word:

"God is not a man, that He should lie, nor a son of man that He should change His mind. Does He speak and then not act? Does He promise and not fulfill?" *(Numbers 23:19).*

Because I know God is faithful, not in theory but experientially, I continued to do the natural things and left the supernatural to God who was the initiator of the program.

CHAPTER FOUR

SEIZING OPPORTUNITIES FOR SUCCESS

T here is indeed a time for everything, and a season for every activity under heaven, *"A time to weep and a time to laugh, a time to mourn and a time to dance"* (Eccl. 3: 1;4). Through this journey of faith, I continue to learn vital lessons that can help you, who is reading this book. God may speak to you or give you an idea — instead of praying for God to manifest it, YOU have to take action to prepare yourself or to make room to actualize what God has spoken. When I was the Ranger of the Girl Scouts in Secondary school, our Motto was: "Be Prepared" not to do things according to plan but to seize any opportunity. Goliath would have continued to frighten the Israelites if David did not seize the opportunity (1 Sam. 17:20-32). This is a very important lesson to learn, some success hinges more on unplanned opportunities that are in line with who you are in God.

Many Christians don't experience the end result of what they felt in their spirit because of being too spiritual. They miss opportunities as they continue to pray or fast instead of taking action. If you do not take proper action to implement what you received through a spoken word or through a still small voice in your spirit, nothing would manifest, or it would take a long time for you to realize what you missed. David was not part of Israel's army, one day he heard what provoked and violated his belief and he decided to take action even though it was not approved by anyone. It was just based on what he felt in his spirit and his conscience.

When God instructed me to unite His Body in the DC Metro area, I could have spiritualized it and made it into a prayer point. We could have continued to pray while remaining in our groups or comfort zones without coming together as people of different nations, different tribes and religious backgrounds, though we are one before God. Our prayers could have been powerful but without the manifestation of what was spoken and without pleasing the Father's heart. Instead, I left my comfort zone, ignored all the criticisms, even from people I respected and loved in order to obey what God instructed me to do. I also had to lay down my own fear of wondering

"What would people say should the meeting fail?" I couldn't shake off the "What-if syndrome." Nevertheless, I had to encourage myself and give myself a small talk, "Who cares if people talk, they talked about Jesus and He continued to fulfill what He came to do."

Sometimes this small talk can be a hinderance or an encouragement, depending how you use them. On that day, I knew no one would kill me for my faith to obey God, so I had no excuse to disobey Him. It takes courage to do what is not approved by others, it takes courage to obey God when you have no idea if what you are asked to do will work or not. It takes courage to be committed to be Christ-like these days.

It is the trick of the enemy to put thoughts in your mind and turn your focus on the dispiriting things your friends, family or community say about you living a life dedicated to obeying God, to worry that you would be left out of some of their activities. Do not worry because you and God are the majority and a day of reward is going to come. Above all, be thankful because you are not being persecuted for your faith like other nations. In the New Testament, the Book of Acts, the Apostles were brought before the Sanhedrin to be told not to preach in the name of Jesus. Many suffered death because of their faith — Conflict with the world and its authorities is sometimes inevitable for a Christian. There would be situations where you have to choose to obey God or to obey men. If you read the speech of Peter, knowing that the leaders had power to imprison them, with courage he still refused to obey their ungodly commands, instead he said, *"…we must obey God rather than men."* (Acts 5:29). This should be our response as well.

God's Ways are Above Cultural Ways

Let me expound more about a story I've shared early on. This Bible narrative fascinates me. A shepherd boy named David was always forgotten by his family, he was the last one to know of any important family meeting, he was the errand boy. One day, his father sent him to take food supplies to his brothers who were at the war front, he willingly obeyed his father and went. Young David was just running an ordinary errand for his father, but when he arrived at the war front, he saw a problem that the army could not solve. He became curious and started asking questions. When his older brother saw David talking to the soldiers, he became angry and scorned David to the point of insulting him publicly, *"I know how conceited you are and how wicked your heart is,"* Eliab *said to David.* Imagine; what you would have done if you were publicly insulted by a member of your family like what David's older brother did? In my culture, if I were David, I would have had to obey my brother and return home quickly. In fact, if I were David, I would have had to apologize for talking to the elders without permission.

Although God created culture, David had a revelation that God was above culture, that is why David did not listen to his brother, instead he went to speak to someone else who listened to the strategy on how to solve the problem at hand. Unfortunately, everybody who heard him told David it was "impossible", even King Saul reminded David that he was only a boy who was too young to fight in a war. But David was not an ordinary boy, in his lonely times, when there was no one to play with him because he had to be on the desert to take care of his father's sheep, David developed an intimate relationship with God. God was his closest friend and companion; they had an intimate relationship that did not need many words but action! Even on the day that he went to visit his brothers, David was not alone there. I imagine when they were speaking so negatively, David was tuning to the frequencies of heaven to hear instructions and he heard his best friend whisper in his spirit, how he could solve the problem by using a sling shot. Indeed, David brought victory to Israel by using a "foolish" strategy (Read 1 Samuel 17:12-51).

Like David, I was clear that God had spoken and given me a simple strategy even though I did not understand what it all meant. I am, today, still confident in this strategy that God showed me in 1993 and He continues to speak about it. Now I have a better understanding as this strategy is working in the lives and communities of all those who have embraced it. Therefore, I am convinced this strategy will work, embrace it, you have nothing to lose. God spoke to me audibly. It was like someone holding my neck and saying, "November 20, start uniting Christians to pray and claim Africa!" It was so clear, I heard HIM and all my stubbornness dissolved. I obeyed without any clue as to what it entailed, that was in 1993. Today, I encourage Christians of every denomination around the world to try, take a step of faith, test God through His revealed word and strategy by uniting for the sake of your community.

Since the instruction was to pray for every country and its president, I had to contact the African Embassies in Washington DC and invite them using this simple message, "Ambassador, as you serve your nations politically, economically and socially, know there are people who will be praying for you, your President and his government as well as praying for the people of your nation. We represent your country spiritually because we know God is the only one who has strategies to solve problems, to bless and prosper you. We therefore invite you and your diplomatic staff to come for these special prayers...."

I remember one day when I called an embassy to ask for the name of their president, the man who spoke with me said, "You sound as if you are from Africa, why do you want to know the president of our country? You are the people foreign governments use to bring confusion in Africa." The person's words pierced my spirit; I felt hurt, insulted, discouraged and I wanted to quit. But God and His gentle spirit encouraged me to keep on making the preparations (In those days there were political unrests and coups in several African countries).

Keep Going Despite the Obstacles

No matter what comes my way I try to remind myself with this thought, *'If Jesus, who was righteous was misunderstood, how much more a mere person like me.'* It is okay to face challenges and not to allow the challenges to hinder your destiny. As the Word says,

> *"A student is not above his teacher, nor a servant above his master. It is enough for the student to be like his teacher, and the servant like his master, If the head of the house has been called Beelzebub, how much more the members of his household! (Matthew: 10: 24-25)*

Indeed, there are several places in the Word of God where Jesus was called Beelzebub, the prince of demons (Matthew 12:24; Mark 3:22). Such awareness and knowledge from the Word should energize and keep you going to fulfill your destiny in spite of the daily obstacles. In fact, learn to use obstacles as stepping stones to go up to where you want to go like Jesus did.

Although I purposed to organize the meeting that had never been held before, I still had thoughts of "what if" in my mind, so I wanted to have the assurance and laid a fleece before God like Gideon did, *"….give me a sign to know it is really you talking to me… (Judges 6:17, 37)*. I told God if He really wanted to use me to encourage unity in the Body of Christ, He had to prove it by bringing at least 12 leaders from different countries, denominations and ministries on the day of the prayer meeting. If people from different places and different backgrounds come, then I would know He indeed spoke and He was serious about seeing unity of His people expressed for the world to believe that Jesus is Lord.

A day before the meeting, I blocked all distractions and fear; I kept thanking God for surprising me and the DC Metro area with a great turnout. That sense of anticipating a supernatural intervention did not leave my mind. I was optimistic because I knew He spoke and He never fails to deliver. On the day He instructed, November 20, we started our first Africa for Jesus Prayer Meeting in Silver Spring. It was beautiful and overwhelming, over 150 people from different nations, churches, denominations and ministries were in attendance. I gave the list of nations and their presidents to Senior Pastors and Diplomats from several embassies who had a relationship with Christ so that they could lead us in prayers.

On that day, everything that was done was very specific to God's instruction for the day. We prayed and declared for war and coups to cease in Africa; for famine and political unrest to be a thing of the past. We declared the children of Africa to prosper and those in the diaspora not to forget where they came from. We prayed for desires to arise in their hearts to connect with their home of origin and start doing something to help change the misery in Africa. People sincerely prayed and were moved by the power of God's presence. The unity of His Body was a testimony to everyone in attendance, it gave them hope and courage to claim Africa and America for Jesus and to know that they are in America for a mission to always pray for this great nation and bring spiritual and moral revival.

I hope you are imagining what was going on in my mind. I felt very fulfilled, in fact I somehow felt vindicated because of the success of the meeting. All those who mocked me and said it was impossible, were witnesses and became part of bringing practical unity of the Body of Christ in the DC Metro area. No wonder the Psalmist said, *"You prepare a table before me in the presence of my enemies. You anoint my head with oil, my cup overflows"* (Ps. 23:5). That day I silently continued to thank God for helping me to do what seemed an impossible task.

Arguing with God in Church!

Just before the last prayer, I heard God saying audibly in my ears, "Next month do the same thing." I also refused audibly and said, "No, not again!" The pastor who sat near me turned to see if I was talking to him and asked, "What, Dr. Mordi?" I apologetically answered him and said, "Sorry, I was thinking aloud!" After a few minutes, I heard again, "In December, continue like today!" As a human, I was so upset to hear anything more from GOD! I know it sounds bad, but that is how I felt! I was upset. And I think my frustration drew on my face because the MC kept looking at me as if to ask, "Dr. Mordi, do you need anything? Or do you want me to say anything?" I am sure those in leadership, especially if you sit on the stage or in the front row, there are some unspoken cues that are exchanged on or from platforms. The MC kept looking at me but I did not pay any attention to him, I was too busy arguing with God in my mind and spirit. It was hard for me to accept to continue for another month because when He first told me, He did not tell me this was a monthly assignment!

Moreover, it was hard because when I was inviting people for the November 20 meeting, I told them it was a onetime event of practical unity. Africans and Friends of Africa from different nations and backgrounds were to pray and claim Africa for Jesus, as well as pray for America and other nations. I did not tell them it was going to be a monthly program. My frustration was also about the facility we used. I could not do it again in December because I requested the use of the church for one Saturday only, November 20. To be told to continue, was not fair; I did not want to embarrass myself to ask for another month. Can you believe how selfish I was, I should have counted it an honor to be chosen by God for such a noble task. However, I now know it was my ego that wanted me to disobey God. Thank God for the Holy Spirit who continued to urge me to do it again in December, so I had to yield and ignore all what was going on in my flesh about being embarrassed before the community.

Agree with His Word Despite Challenges

I got courage and leaned towards Pastor Johnson and apologetically whispered in his ears and said, "Sorry Pastor, I told you it was a one-day prayer gathering but now God wants us to come back in December and I am not sure what to do. Do you think we can come back next month?" He did not say anything except turn away after I finished speaking. My mind was going in different directions instead of focusing on what was going on the last few minutes of the program. Pastor Johnson, as the host pastor, was called to give final remarks and a closing prayer. I became attentive to what he was going to say. As soon as he took the mic, he thanked everyone for coming and said, "This is a powerful symbol of unity, no one came here to pray for their churches or ministries but to pray for nations and their leaders. This is pleasing to God, but before I close in prayer and give the benediction, Dr. Mordi has an announcement to make." He calmly and diplomatically handed me the microphone.

With a big smile I stood and echoed my gratitude for all who came and thanked Rev Dr. Johnson and his leadership team for allowing nations to gather in their facility. Then I added, "When I was preparing this service and inviting you to come, I told most of you the meeting was going to be a one-time event. However, while we were singing the last song, God said we should come back in December at the same time. I pray you felt the presence of God as we all united for His agenda and you can agree that we have to come back next month. How many of you believe we need to continue next month?" Almost all the hands went up, then I confidently added, "Please inform others to come and represent their nations, thank you so much for being here. May God continue to use you."

I thanked all the Senior Pastors and the diplomates who lead the prayers. The South African political refugee who lead us in the South African national anthem — Khosi Sikeleli Africa. I thanked Minister Helen who led us in songs and praises, also in singing the Swahili National Anthem of Tanzania which is a prayer and declaration of blessings upon Africa and her people. Lastly, I turned around to the host Pastor, Rev. Dr. Johnson to give him the microphone and a hug by adding these words, "We appreciate you for opening your church to host this historic meeting to unite Christians of different countries, ethnic groups and denominations to pray for the entire continent and the USA. Thank you. We were all blessed to sing in Swahili. We thank God for your desire to host again next month, may God bless you and prosper your entire Bethel family".

We ended the meeting with excitement and it was the talk of the community. People looked forward to the next meeting. Indeed, on the Third Saturday of December, we met again. More people came and different pastors and expatriates were given the list to read and pray over every country, every president, called every U.S. State and declared Africa and America for Jesus. Though Africa was the focus we prayed for Israel and the entire world.

That day the leadership team felt fulfilled knowing we had done what God required us to do. After we finished, I started preparing for the Christmas holidays with joy and satisfaction about the two meetings we held to pray for nations. It felt good knowing I indeed heard from God who still speaks like He did in the Old Testament, *"Then the word of the Lord came to Jeremiah "I am the Lord, the God of all mankind. Is anything too hard for me?" (Jeremiah 32:26-27)* Indeed, there is nothing too hard for Jehovah.

We celebrated the New Year with church friends in our home without any thought that I would have to mobilize people to continue the united prayers to claim Africa and America for Jesus and other nations in subsequent years. I love to pray for nations but I did not like the specificity of how to do it, if someone else was going to continue, that would have been okay, I did not want it to be me.

CHAPTER FIVE

GOD'S FINGER ON MY BEDROOM WALL

There was excitement about the New Year with a fresh feeling of gratitude for all that God did in the previous year. Before day break on Monday, January 3, 1994, I was still enjoying my sleep in my bed, then I saw a strange bright beam of light cast in my bedroom. Without any warning, God literary woke me up and gave me instructions saying, "Write these dates down and continue to pray for the nations as I commanded you to do last year!" "Excuse me; is it a joke?" these words of unbelief I thought to myself. I wiped the sleep from my eyes and looked up, but the light was too bright to see anything. I sat down to see if my husband had come home from his night job and had turned on the big light because no one else was at home. I did not see him so I called his name, "George! Are you home?" All was silent and the entire room was bright.

Still sitting on my bed, I carefully looked at the light switch, it was off and the bulbs seemed not to be what was producing the light in the room. The small night light on the wall was the only one that was on. I could not understand why such a bright light filled the room. After a few minutes passed, I concluded that I was only dreaming. I threw my head back on my pillow and pulled my cover over my head and face to block out the light.

Unfortunately, the covers could not block the light and I could not control it. Then the voice again said, "Write those dates down and continue to pray for the nations as I instructed you to do before." The voice filled the entire room, I quickly removed the cover from my face, wiping my eyes one more time. I did not see anything at all, so I sat up to look around. As I looked, I saw my bedroom wall as if it was painted dark. Again, I wiped my eyes properly, this time I even stretched my neck and opened my eyes wide for clearer vision. What I saw was unbelievable, almost crazy! My bedroom wall was covered with dates from January 1994 to December 2006 plus other figures I could not see. My mouth was left ajar, one hand covered it to prevent myself from screaming. I really did not know what to think or say. I was in shock. At that moment, I knew for sure that I was wide awake and not dreaming. I stared at the wall and looked in bewilderment! Then I felt a push and a command for the third time, "Copy those dates and continue to pray for the nations".

Unfortunately, I cannot put words to all that went on in my entire being. How I got the legal pad and started copying the dates down, I do not remember. Until now I cannot say if I got it myself or some angel on assignment handed it to me — I cannot tell, nor can I tell where the pad came from. However, I recall holding the pad and thinking, these are too many dates — it was from 1994 to 2006, all together was 12 years. These 12 years did not appear at the same time, I remember first seeing 2000 without paying much attention to the last numbers, and when I started copying the numbers, the hand kept on writing until it reached December 2006, then it did not write any more.

After I finished copying the dates up to 2006, the bright light suddenly disappeared. I yelled on impulse, "What is going on?" In a panic, I looked around but all was calm and quiet. I was trembling — not in fear but in wonder, "What did that visitation really mean?" "What would my husband say if he saw our bedroom wall covered with numbers?" Many different thoughts flashed through my mind. When I came to my right mind, I put the light on to look at the wall, to my surprise, the wall was completely clean, but the pad was on my bed with the numbers written on it. Then reality hit me, and I started weeping, overwhelmed with feelings that I cannot explain. I could not say that they were tears of worship, maybe they were tears of fear from seeing only a hand without a body writing on my wall. I really do not know how to describe that moment, nor could I say it was a visitation from angels but from God, the Son. To say that moment was filled with un explainable shock and an overwhelming mixture of other emotions is more accurate.

My Struggle to Believe

We were in the 20th century. Those things did not happen often. Unfortunately, my weeping and questioning did not bring any clarity to the situation. After tiring myself trying to get clarity and with my mixed emotions, I remembered who I was and made up my mind to focus on worshiping God and hoped it was but a dream and that the pad would disappear by daybreak. I knelt by my bedside and started talking to the only one who knows the end from the beginning. He is the lover of my soul who has all solutions. As I continued to encourage myself, I must have fallen asleep on the carpet, when I woke up, the first thing that I looked for was the pad, not because I wanted to see it, but because I wanted to prove that the encounter of the previous night was just a dream. To my surprise, the pad with the dates was not a dream but a reality. God's finger had written those dates on my bedroom wall and He had commanded me to copy them. He wanted me to be a spokesperson who received those dates, months and years in order to remind Christians to foster unity to claim and pray for the nations on those dates.

I was not eager to share with the ministry leadership team what God showed me. I wanted to ponder some more. The experience was too unreal for anyone to understand except for the evidence of the dates that everyone could see. But still, I did not have the energy to talk about it. I can't recall how many days passed before I took the pad and shared with the Board and team members what I had written on it and what God had said. They all agreed that we had to obey God and continue to unite His Body to pray for the nations. Then I requested one of the faithful servants of God, Sister Helen Asifiri, to put up a praise team from different churches who would lead during these prayers. She did an excellent job forming a group of what we called The Highest Praise Team Singers and Musicians from different churches and nations willingly gathering to lead the multination's team of singers before the united Body of Christ started the intercessory prayers.

Don't Sacrifice Purpose for Activities

Those days, many people looked forward to be part of the Third Saturday Prayers that united His Body. For several months it did not occur to us to find out the importance of that specific day the prayers were held, nor do I remember asking God what was special about the dates He wrote on my bedroom wall. I was caught up in the fact that I saw dates written by an invisible hand — it was a big deal that could not get out of my mind. Other details were not in my mind at all. I was consumed by the reality that "GOD wrote on my bedroom wall!" Although I knew the Old Testament tells of a similar encounter God had in the 6th century BC with a powerful ruler of Babylon, this happening in my house in the 20th century was totally different and supernatural. Many people do not experience miracles so they assume miracles are over. In the experience of King Belshazzar when he saw the hand writing, his loins were loosed and his knees knocked one against another. If the king felt that way in his palace, surrounded by people, imagine what I might have gone through. The Bible says,

> *"Suddenly the fingers of a human hand appeared and wrote on the plaster of the wall, near the lampstand in the royal palace. The king watched the hand as it wrote. His face turned pale and he was so frightened that his legs became weak and his knees were knocking. (Daniel 5:5-6).*

Today however, it is easy to understand because of technology. Technology makes it possible to have a hand write on a board. But in 1994, there was no such technology, especially in my neighborhood or in my circles. Even if it was available, and could be done at night, it did not happen in a conference room or a classroom, but on the wall of my bedroom. Moreover, what was written, dates 12 years in advance, is a proof that no human intellect was involved. That phenomenon was a supernatural miracle then, and it is still a supernatural miracle today.

CHAPTER SIX

TEXAS RECEIVES SAME REVELATION

A s I was preparing for the service one day in March, I heard a whisper in my spirit, "Check what day you are supposed to pray?" Within myself, a response came immediately with an explanation, "It is a Saturday because it is the day convenient for people to come together." Then again, I heard, "No, it is not any Saturday but the *Third Saturday*." I jacked up and said a big, "Eh!" because it did not make sense. How did **Third Saturday** come into the picture? Who was counting? After being bewildered for a while, the spirit of understanding came over me and I started checking the dates more closely. Surprisingly, all the dates from the first day that the Lord spoke concerning the prayer to be held, November 20, 1993 to the dates that the writing appeared on my bedroom wall, when I looked at them carefully, all the dates were the **Third Saturdays of each month**. Immediately I remembered the scripture that says, *"This is what we speak, not in words taught us by human wisdom, but in words taught by the Spirit, expressing spiritual truth in spiritual words,"* (I Cor. 2:13).

Paul wrote this scripture to assure Christians in Corinth that he was not writing his personal views or impressions of what God said but that the source of what he was writing was directly from the Holy Spirit. I am trying to convey to Christians today, the need to pray and how to pray on the Third Saturday of each month. The fact that it is not my idea but a directive from God through the Holy Spirit who desire His Body — with the many different parts take the Third Saturday to pray and declare Kingdom agenda anywhere they are.

Unaffected by the Y2K Anxiety

Months before the end of 1999, controversy arose about the new millennium. Many had sleepless nights about what might happen before they crossed over to the New Year of 2000. Some even said it might be the end of the world — It was called, "The Y2K Fever." The thought of it brought panic and paralyzed many. In the age of computers and advanced technology, scientists did not have a clue of how the astronomical system would change to the new year. The world was in panick about whether there would be a computer crash, that meant no selling or buying of anything. Many churches were telling people to stock necessary items for survival just in case! Some prophets urged people to look for places to hide for shelter and to stock up on non-perishable goods.

Thanks be to God that fear was not a concern to those who were part of the Third Saturday United Prayers. I had the confidence and the direction of the Holy Spirit to tell them what they were saying was not true and they should not spread fear to the masses because 2000 was going to be like any other New Year. The only person who knows the end from the beginning is God, and He is the one who wrote correct days and dates 12 years in advance to share with His Children (1994-2006). Even experts in calendrical matters, cannot compare to the wisdom and knowledge of God. If He wrote the dates, then we were certainly going to accomplish what He said we should accomplish until 2006. I advised Children of God not to buy into fear that was propagated by people of the world. We must always depend on God because He alone is the Alpha and Omega, the Beginning and the end. Also, in you is the deposit of His divine nature that is filled with power and sound mind.

After being told it was not an ordinary day, I discussed with the Africa for Jesus leadership team asking what all that meant? What is the Third Saturday and why? No one seemed to know except to encourage ourselves to be faithful to what God had said and started. Sometimes

Sister Helen and I would discuss and say different things like maybe it is the sign of the Trinity, or maybe it signifies the resurrection day, when Christ arose on the Third day. In reality, I did not fully understand what the significance of the Third "Day" represented. We just knew that we needed to obey what God had commanded and involve the entire Body of Christ.

We obeyed blindly and continued to unite on the third Saturday of every month to pray very specifically for nations and their leaders. We prayed against political unrest in Africa, against all that was not good for the people: poverty, corruption, diseases and injustice. We were very focused and the leaders who were chosen to read the names and the prayer points were all done according to the Word of God. Every time we met, people felt that it was indeed a God-given mandate because no one was involved in selfish prayers but all was kingdom focused, for communities and nations to experience God's love and unity.

Texas sends Flag Revelation

After sometime, I received a large package from Texas. When I opened the package, I was shocked by the content. It was a praying for Africa poster board that someone had painted. We had never met, but she had her own encounter with the Holy Spirit. She sent a message telling me of how God had awakened her and told her to paint the board and send it to I GO Ministries because they were the people who were assigned to pray and bring unity for Africa. This poster board was painted in five colors; she was told that those were African colors. In the center, it was written "Praying for Africa" in big black colors. When I saw it, and read the note, I had goose bumps all over and tears rolled down my cheeks. I was in awe of how much God was concerned to make sure different people of every race have a part to play to unite His Body. Above all, I was in awe of how He could speak to a white American lady in Texas to affirm what God had spoken in the Washington Metropolitan area concerning Africa for Jesus prayer unity and declaration. It was beyond my comprehension.

I could no longer question or doubt what I was doing because everything about this movement of Praying for Africa and other nations began supernaturally and that is how it has been to now. None of it was my idea. When the ministry Board and team leaders saw the poster board, they were shocked as well and agreed that it should be used as a prayer contact for the nations. Each time we met on the Third Saturday of every month to pray in one accord, the person leading prayer for a designated region, would lay hands on that miracle poster board and call the name of every president and declare each country and her leaders in North, East, West and South Africa for Jesus.

Sometimes all the leaders would go up and lay hands on the board at the same time. When we prayed for America, we called all 50 states by name and the President in DC. We would use the American flag as the point of contact for this nation and for the world. What happens in America affects the entire world, so we prayed that God's righteousness would penetrate every system of power, the Judiciary, the Legislature and the Executive Branch so that in God they would truly trust and advance His Kingdom lifestyle. As I write this book, disunity and hate has increased in America because the Church refused to include this simple strategy in their many meetings of prayers. God is not moved by status quo but by obedience.

After 12 months of consistent united prayers, we held the first anniversary of the Third Saturday United Prayer at the Holiday Inn downtown Washington DC. That meeting brought together many well-known individuals in the Body of Christ, such as Archbishop Nicholas Duncan Williams from Ghana and Bishop Gary McIntosh from Tulsa, Oklahoma as our first anniversary speakers, and many more. Our theme was, "God is Up to Something". We invited different church choirs and musicians including traditional Christian dances, diplomats, expatriates and the Mayor of Washington DC.

The celebrations started Wednesday night and concluded Saturday night. Some of these details are vital to inform the reader and the public about how this Third Saturday Unity Prayer movement started — It is not my vision or ministry as many think, but God who used me as His prophet for the unity of His Body. It is to also convince you and many others to include the Third Saturday Prayer in their programs to declare God's kingdom agenda to be fulfilled in every family, community and nation.

On that first anniversary, in the capital city of the most powerful nation in the world, history was made by the diaspora, not for any political agenda, but to acknowledge that only God has power over the nations and the story of Africa would change because the people of Africa are arising.

The Spirit of God leads Daily. Depend on Him

Before our second anniversary, I heard in my spirit that I should contact people from Ethiopia to also get involved because all African countries have their headquarters in Ethiopia, Addis Ababa called the OAU (Organization of Africa Union). It is possible you are not used to hearing someone say they heard the Spirit telling them or they follow the leading of the Holy Spirit like I have been saying. My life is by faith and I totally depend on the leading the Spirit of God. Since I was young, I have tried to do His will, I trust Him completely and my life is totally surrendered to obey and to do His will. I try to obey even if I don't understand what God wants me to do. The Psalmist says,

"the Lord delights in the life of the man whose steps he has made firm, though he stumbles, he will

not fall, for the Lord upholds him with his hand."
(Psalm 37:23-24).

Another scripture that I want to share with you as an encouragement to live by is what David said in Proverbs 3:5-6. *"Trust in the Lord with all your heart and lean not on your own understanding. In all your ways acknowledge Him and He will make your paths straight."* Those who feel the Christian life is hard is because they hardly read the Word of God to find out such great promises of God directing your paths instead of depending on yourself. Let this not be a reality in your Christian journey.

Totally depending on God's leading started in my early Christian life when He called me as a young girl. Through personal experience I learned how to hear His voice in different ways. I wish I could share with you all about these 54 years of walking with Him, hearing Him and serving Him by serving His people by faith; it has been very fulfilling. I wish I could say I never doubt or question when He speaks. Sometimes I totally miss what He is saying because of doubt. Nevertheless, I am filled with joy when I know I have obeyed and what He told me comes to pass. Some of these experiences are written in my book, "Blind Faith: God's Amazing Miracles" with the foreword written by my mentor Oral Roberts who was a personal friend, and more so his wife, Evelyn Roberts. One day I will publish another book with

Roberts personal letter to me and many more great men of God in our generation.

We often prayed together with Evelyn Roberts, especially when I had an important upcoming mission trip. Even when they left Tulsa, OK and moved to California, I would call her at their home on Grandville Drive in New Port Beach, California, and ask her to continue to pray for me while I was gone. In fact, few days before she passed away, we spoke because I was about to travel to Africa, she told me about her dental appointment and asked me to pray that all would go well — that was where she fell and never recovered. Bishop Johnson called me while I was still in Nigeria to tell me about her death, I was devastated. Evelyn Roberts truly cared and respected who I am as a strong prayer warrior. From time to time she would send me letters of encouragement. When she could not write, she would dictate to her daughter Robertta who sent me the letters on behalf of her mother. I thank God for surrounding me with such great men and women of faith, they are irreplaceable.

When God told me to contact the Ethiopian people. I started looking in the Yellow Pages but I only saw Ethiopian Orthodox Churches. My spirit did not feel right. Then out of the blue, I felt the spirit saying, "Look for Evangelical Churches." As children of God, we must depend on the Holy Spirit within to guide and direct us, that is the major reason He came. Jesus said,

"But when he, the Spirit of truth, comes, he will guide you into all the truth. He will not speak on his own; he will speak only what he hears, and he will tell you what is yet to come. (John 16:13).

This is the life I have chosen to live — a life of total dependence on Him. As I obeyed His simple leading, I found an Ethiopian Evangelical Church located in Washington, DC. I took the number and immediately called them. It was busy but I kept calling and telling the Lord, "If they answer, let me get an appointment with the pastor," that was my desire and it was what I spoke as I kept calling. Finally, the secretary answered. She said the pastor had no opening for three weeks and I should call after that. I asked, "When do you have your services?" she replied, "We have one tonight." "Is the pastor going to be there?" I asked. She said, "Yes!" I thanked her and hung up the phone quickly because I had a plan to execute.

I took the Yellow Pages again and looked for the address. I was not familiar with Washington, DC, but I was determined to go to the church and attend their service. Meanwhile, I called my husband at work and told him to cancel everything that evening so he could go to DC with me. When he asked about the details, I just told him it was very important. He was tired and he really did not want to go, but I was determined to go with him as a witness to partake of the blessings of an assignment from

God. I knew God had directed me to them. I told my husband this time I could not take his no for an answer. Above all, he knew when he says he is tired, I normally would leave him alone. However, he felt it was unusual for me to keep on insisting that he go with me, so he finally agreed to go but would not drive.

When we got there, the service had already begun. We sat at the back not hearing anything they were saying and my husband asked why I had dragged him there. It did not matter to me that we were not hearing anything because my purpose for being there was not necessarily to listen to their service. As we sat in the service, my eyes scanned the beautiful facility; I was in awe of how large and impressive the building was, I admired the high painted ceiling and was filled with joy. After a while, I turned and poked my husband a little and said, "George, God has given this facility to us, we would use it for our 2nd anniversary services in November." As usual, my husband turned to me with that look and said, "Nicku, stop your craziness, you have not spoken with the pastor, this is your first time calling the office and you are already talking nonsense." I did not pay any attention to what he was saying but continued in confidence, "I know what the spirit told me when the secretary said the pastor would be at the service tonight. Sitting in this church, I know that God has already given it to us, they just don't know it yet." I said it with a smile on my face because I was very serious, using that church was already a reality. "But Nicku, you did not even have an appointment with him, you have just shown up and dragged me here for the service, now you say you have the building?" My husband doubted. He turned away and didn't want to be bothered with my day dreaming.

At that moment, I did not consider his comments but continued to rejoice and visualize how we would decorate the place with national flags of countries in Africa and other nations. I was so convinced because the idea of looking for an Ethiopian Church did not come from me but from the Spirit of God, therefore, I had no business doubting that God would not do it. He had given us many promises, like when He said, *"if you remain (abide) in me and my words remains in you, ask whatever you wish, and it will be given you" (John 15:7)*. I had asked and He gave me His word and that was the basis of my unwavering faith. Indeed, through continuous hunger to commune with Him, you start learning to hear Him clearly. John 10:27 says, *"My sheep listen to my voice, I know them, and they follow me."*

Unison in the Spirit

As soon as the service was over, I said to my husband, "George, let's go to the front and meet the pastor". My husband's look said a thousand words and then he said, "You go yourself; you will find me here." I left him and walked to the front with a smile in my heart. As soon as I had opportunity to talk with the pastor, I introduced myself and said directly, "I came because we want to use your church for the Africa For Jesus second anniversary prayer service." Without any hesitation he said, "You know we moved to this location just two months ago, we are still new in this sanctuary." As soon as I heard him say they just moved, I said to him, "Pastor, you moved here because God knew His daughter would be coming to request you for your facilities to be involved in the Africa for Jesus prayer service in November." He agreed without any question or hesitation. He told me to come back and give them the dates and what I wanted to see happen.

You can imagine how I felt as I walked back to my husband. I was on cloud nine ready to say, "YOU SEE! Nothing is impossible with God," but I did not have to say anything, the expression on my face said everything. "You got it!" He asked, I answered him with a thumbs up. I was ecstatic because God had given us the best place that became our Spiritual Organization of African Unity (OAU). If I had waited to call back as the secretary had suggested, we could have missed God's favor. I seized the opportunity and the outcome was miraculous. Since that day in 1995 until today, the International Ethiopian Evangelical Church of Washington, DC with Pastor Hanfere Aligaz as Senior Pastor has hosted meetings and anniversaries for the Unity of the Body of Christ Prayer movement.

To this day, Rev. Aligaz is on the executive advisory board and one of his assistant pastors, Rev. Abtew Kebede is the Africa for Jesus United Prayer Movement executive coordinator for the United States. God connected us for Kingdom purposes and it is amazing how He continues to guide and direct what we have to do regarding this simple strategy for His Kingdom agenda. We have travelled in many different nations to teach Church leaders on sustainable strategies to transform nations. The more we promote the Third Saturday unity, the Body of Christ understands and see the need to obey this divine strategy. To be part of an end-time spiritual revival to impact nations is not an easy task, but it is worthy of all our efforts and participation to make it work.

CHAPTER SEVEN

NIGERIA CHOSEN FIRST

God's universal mandate does not appear to only one person. He speaks to several people in different parts of the world. It is up to those individuals to obey God to do whatever is possible to accomplish the assignment then God will start connecting these people to accomplish a bigger agenda. The Unity Prayer was revealed to, besides me, a woman in Texas who was told of what to do to enhance the mandate of Praying for Africa. In Africa, God started showing visions to individuals about a woman in America who was carrying Africa to the cross of Jesus while others were being mandated to look for me. I know there are many people who have been told the same thing, on the same Third Saturday we can unite and spread a spiritual quilt of many colors and patterns for end-time harvest. The harvest is ready,

God's Spirit is moving all over the world, it is up to Church leaders to expand their vision to accommodate the kingdom harvest.

Before the 1999 Thanksgiving holiday, God said in my spirit, "Take the Third Saturday Prayer Unity mandate to Africa!" This time, I was not sure if it would still be held on the third Saturday because people were consumed with the Y2K hype. Nevertheless, I told the Chairman of the Board that we needed to think about introducing this mandate to the continent of Africa. However, I added that I had no idea which country to start with or how to choose the first one. I asked him to pray for clear direction. He reminded me of how I told him the movement would be beneficial to bring Africans, who normally would not be invited by large organizations, to attend conferences in the United States.

Indeed, that is what I believed and that was what we did for the past anniversaries. We invited Christians from around the world who could afford to come to Washington, DC to attend the Africa for Jesus celebration. Every November, Christians in the DC Metropolitan area eagerly anticipated the anniversary celebrations. God promised to do the supernatural if Christians would unite to pray and claim their families, nations and continents for His glory. Indeed, every November we experienced unity of Africans and friends of Africa who filled the Ethiopian Evangelical Church in Washington, DC. I had no intention of interrupting what was a supernatural move of united prayers to take it anywhere else. Nonetheless, obeying His leading was a priority. I shared with the leadership team as well as my pastor, asking for prayers and clarity as to which country we should go first.

It is in my nature to place my whole heart with what the Holy Spirit instructs me to do. I knew it was God who wanted us to go to Africa, but I had no idea where or which country, so I had to share with the leadership team because the Word of God says, *"For lack of guidance a nation falls, but victory is won through many advisers" (Proverbs 11:14).* As I talked to them about the third Saturday mandate in Africa and which country to go first, I could sense the leaders had no problem with the idea. Nevertheless, I kept pondering over it in my heart, waiting to hear a final direction from God. At the same time, a lingering thought in me wondered if those dates God wrote on the wall would still be the Third Saturday even in the new millennium.

God's Word is Fulfilled

The year 2000 arrived and the computers did not crash as feared. No wonder the acronym for FEAR is False Evidence Appearing Real. For months, many people benefited by planting fear in people's minds to buy and prepare for the unknown. Fortunately, the new year came just like any other year and the dates remained the same as was given in 1994. Indeed, God controls everything and His revealed word protected us from the Y2K madness. We continued to unite the Body of Christ to claim Africa, America and other nations for Jesus. Although it was and still is a great challenge because of the enormity of the task, we still have to totally depend on God and trust Him to lead us one step after another. I was confident of what God spoke about because our focus was to motivate others so that Jesus alone would be exalted and His children were being encouraged to say "Jesus is Lord" everywhere they went.

A few months after the instruction to go to Africa came, I heard our Church was planning a trip to Liberia for the consecration ceremony for the Bishop of Bethel World Outreach Ministries International, Rev. Dr. Darlingston Johnson who was also the I GO Africa for Jesus Chairman. By then I was serving as the Executive Assistant to the Bishop of the church, as well as the International Missions Director, so I had to be part of the trip to Liberia. I could have taken that as a sign for us to start the Third Saturday Prayer Unity in Liberia but I did not because God did not say anything about it.

Meanwhile, I continued to trust God to show us which country in Africa we should start with. Through this journey of faith, my focus was not to do things for God but rather to allow God to do His will through me. This meant being sensitive and obedient to flow with the Holy Spirit's directions. I aspire to obey Him and do things according to His instructions even if it does not make sense. Going to Liberia, I could have easily concluded that the trip was God's way of opening the door to confirm what He had told me to do. But since I did not receive any confirmation from Him or a clear sense in my spirit, I knew that Liberia would not be where we would first introduce the Third Saturday Prayer mandate.

God's Envoy from Akure, Nigeria

We arrived in Monrovia, Liberia excited for the great task ahead of us, Rev. Dr. Darlingston Johnson was being ordained as the Bishop of Bethel World Outreach Ministries International and as his executive assistant, I had several tasks that kept me busy and focused. On the second day of our conference, I was called by the protocol officer and was told that there were people looking for me outside. I requested that he bring them to where we were eating. He said, "No, Dr. Mordi, they cannot come in because they have been driving for five days from Nigeria to Liberia to look for you." I was puzzled because I could not imagine anyone coming to look for me in Liberia. I took my handbag and followed him outside.

As we arrived outside where they were waiting, one of the two men said, "Madam, are you Dr. Mordi?" I politely answered "Yes!" but in my mind I wondered, "Who are these people? What do they want with me?" As I stretched out my hand to greet them, one of them hugged me and said, "Praise God, we are meeting you in person for real." He was excited and genuinely happy to see me though he looked very tired. I was puzzled; many thoughts ran through my mind. Then I heard his friend also echo, "Praise God bishop, now it is for real she is here, it was good we obeyed the Holy Spirit to leave Akure!" Then the man said, "Madam, are you the one God gave a mandate of Africa for Jesus to unite the Body of Christ?" I answered, "Yes!" His face lit up and he continued, "God commanded us to leave Akure, Nigeria to come to look for you in Liberia because He wants you to come to Nigeria with the Africa for Jesus mandate to unite His Body. The Apostle also confirmed it, that is why we came without being sure we would find you."

When I heard those words, my mind rushed in different directions and my heart throbbed within me because God was confirming what He had been saying for over two years. With a polite shout I answered him and said, "Sir, sorry I forgot your name! but what you just said is a confirmation of what God has been saying and I have been waiting for His confirmation on where to go. Now it is confirmed and we will come to Akure, Nigeria. You will have to excuse me, I need to go inside and tell the chairman that God has answered our prayers, thank you for being here."

Because of excitement, I do not recall if I said a proper goodbye to end the conversation, nor did I ask them where they were lodging since they had been driving day and night to locate me. Unfortunately, that did not seem to matter at that moment. What was urgent for me was to tell my Bishop.

With that thought in my mind, I rushed inside where I left Bishop Johnson eating with the others. I could not wait, nor did I apply proper protocol except to excitedly tell him "Bishop, I was called out because two bishops and others came from Nigeria to tell us that God wants the AFJ Prayer conference to be held in Nigeria next year." He looked a little puzzled and asked, "Who are they? Do you know them?" "Sorry, I don't know them and I forgot their names," I responded and then continued to speak, "but I told them to come for the evening service and left the protocol man talking with them. I assume he has gone to show them where to rest until evening, then I will bring them to you." Quietly he said, "Praise God, he has answered your prayers, we will talk in the evening." Then he went to join those who were waiting for him.

Wow, Precision of the Holy Spirit!

After the evening service, we met them and I politely asked for their names again so I could properly introduce them to Bishop Johnson. The head of the delegation was Bishop Michael Adesua of the Cornerstone New Life Church of Akure, Ondo State, Nigeria. Accompanying him was his apostle and another pastor. I took them to a special room where Bishop Johnson was waiting. When we sat together, Bishop Adesua shared how God had instructed him to leave Akure, Nigeria and come to Liberia to look for me and share what God had told them concerning the Africa for Jesus United Prayer Mandate. God wanted Nigeria to be the first country to host the first meeting on the Continent because of the significance of her role for the end-time kingdom agenda.

We were in awe of the precision of the Holy Spirit. Also, no one had ever heard of Akure, yet that was the city God selected to kindle the fire of unity. It reminded me of how the angel of God was sent to Philip and gave him instructions about where he should go to minister to the Ethiopian eunuch. The Bible says, *"An angel of the Lord said to Philip, go south to the road – the desert road – that goes down from Jerusalem to Gaza."* He obeyed and took the road that he was told to take. There he met an Ethiopian eunuch, an important official in charge of all the treasury of Candace, queen of the Ethiopians. Philip did not get all the instructions at once. The Holy Spirit continued to instruct him as he obeyed and took action (Acts 8:26-39). Likewise, these men of God travelled very far. God did not choose a big well-known city but a small city in the densely populated country of Nigeria on the continent of Africa. Indeed, Nigeria is significant for the end-time agenda, God is waiting for their humility to ignite peace and revival across the continent and the world.

Hearing all what God spoke in Akure, it also reminded me of how Bethlehem, a tiny city in Judah, was selected as the birthplace of our Savior.

> *"But you, Bethlehem Ephrathah, though you are small among the clans of Judah, out of you will come for me one who will be ruler over Israel, whose origins are from of old, from ancient times." (Micha 5:2).*

It is also confirmed in the New Testament how God uses those who are weak, unknown, and poor at times; those who are least likely to accomplish what He requires them to do (I Corinthians 1:27-29).

> *"But God choses the foolish things of the world to shame the wise; God chose the weak things of the world to shame the strong, He chooses the lowly things of this world and the despised things – and the things that are not – to nullify the things that are, so that no one may boast before him."*

Bishop Adesua and his team from Akure talked with Bishop Johnson for a while. I left them to take care of other things. Bishop Johnson was moved by their obedience to drive that far without any assurance that I would be there. They demonstrated unshakable faith and the importance of the Third Saturday united Prayer mandate. Bishop Adesua became a team member and was one of those who was part of the consecration team for Bishop Johnson. Indeed, our waiting on God for direction made things much easier because God's ways are the best.

After the consecration, we departed with dates in place; November 14 to 17, 2001 at Akure, Nigeria as the first city and country to host this divine mandate to unite the Body of Christ for end-time impact. Invitations were sent to friends and acquaintances across the Continent. We always tried to involve the entire Body of Christ in our work to "Go into all the world" and to awaken the sleeping giant to arise to her God given responsibility of 'kindomizing' the nations. I am a spokesperson of God's revelation for a specific purpose to benefit everyone who would take action to fulfill this mandate.

Extraordinary Convocation

While we were in Akure, leaders from six different nations came. I remember a young pastor from Tanzania who did not speak any English; he had never travelled outside his country. He felt God wanted him to be part of what He was about to do through the Africa for Jesus convocation. With a step of faith, he left Tanzania and arrived in Lagos without anyone to receive him. His blind faith and determination helped overcome all the chaos of Lagos and he reached Akure supernaturally. We were all amazed at God's grace and travelling mercies. Indeed, any person who dare trust God to do the impossible, will experience the supernatural like this young man, Fauton Ndambila, who is now an influential bishop in his country. He dared to travel to the meeting in Akure that was filled with extraordinary revelations — an indication that this is not an ordinary movement.

We had the privilege to preach in the traditional palace of the king of Akure and many in that compound accepted Jesus and denounced traditional practices and idols. Every night I fell on my knees in awe of God's faithfulness. It is awesome to experience Him anew each day. While in Akure, God whispered in my ears the countries we were to go from 2002 to 2006. He told me to announce the following nations: The Democratic Republic of Congo, Ethiopia, South Africa, Tanzania, and then Liberia. I wondered why Liberia was given 2006 the last year on the divine agenda that He had written in 1994. It would make more sense if we returned to Liberia where God sent the Akure Bishop. God's ways are not our ways. God foresaw what Liberia was about to face and the 2006 prophetic conference was intended to change the spiritual scene in Africa as Liberia was changing the political scene.

Can You Ignore Evidence?

As you read this book, I hope you see God's hand in this movement. It was during the eighth anniversary, the number of new beginnings when we were sent to Nigeria, followed by other significant countries, then God directed us to host a summit in Liberia in 2006 for church leaders from all countries of Africa to deliberate His kingdom agenda, and put Jesus' mission at the center of every message and every program they would hold. At the time, Liberia was at war and leaders discouraged me from including it on the agenda, No one knew if it would be possible for anyone to travel to Liberia. But in 2004 when we were in South Africa, again God sent confirmation, leaders from Liberia came and were ready to host the conference as God told us to do.

Then in 2006, Liberia changed the political scene of Africa by electing the first woman president. Only God knew and had a plan for people to be in Liberia to change the religious climate of Africa. He wanted church leaders and their congregations to focus on Christ and His sacrifice on the cross. The sacrifice which accomplished everything for us. This could be the reason God revealed dates from 1994 to 2006. Having a summit of all leaders to declare nations for Jesus and calling Africa for Jesus was a confession which would allow Jesus to take control of everything in Africa. God's visitation is available if we truly unite as He wants. Unfortunately, people are too busy and too occupied with just a segment of His Body without realizing the malfunction in the entire Body of Christ. Many opportunities are missed because of the blind spot in the Body of Christ. Nonetheless, God continues to wait patiently for His Body to unite. I believe if people everywhere really demonstrated their unity on the third Saturday of every month, many unnecessary church conflicts, tribal wars or racial tensions and political unrests could be avoided and Christians could bring peace in troubling times because Jesus is the Prince of peace.

Every Challenge is an Opportunity

In 2003 God sent us to the war-torn nation of the Democratic Republic of Congo (DRC) to declare peace and encourage those who had been devastated by the war. At the airport the enemy wanted to destroy us. Even when we checked in at our hotel, soldiers came with their machine guns to take us to be interrogated. We could have lost our lives because our host proved to be corrupt, forging all the documents that were sent to us concerning the preparations of the meetings. Bishops and head pastors from different countries of Africa, Europe, and USA could not understand what was happening and why we were detained at the airport. We sent money to book hotels, helped meet the budget for the conference and nothing was done. It was devastating and I was very disappointed with that Bishop.

Nevertheless, my heart was filled with peace and I encouraged the team to remain calm because God had sent us there for a divine purpose, and He would see to it that it was accomplished despite what the devil was trying to do. I told them to see greater opportunity in every obstacle or challenge. Early morning, the army came and took us to the compound for questioning. We were surrounded by more soldiers with machine guns. To make matters worse, they did not allow us to speak with one another. They interrogated us about why we were in the country, I openly shared how God had been sending us to different nations to unite His Body and declare Jesus the Prince of peace to take over that nation. The many boxes we brought were to help the street children and the poor in Kinshasa.

After I finished speaking, God's favor took over, we became the guest of the President. The Secretary of State to the President called all the television stations and the radio stations to interview us. He was touched by our sacrifice to pray for his nation and travel there while it was not safe. He went ahead and gave us the best facility, where the government holds official meetings to use for the AFJ conference. Also, he informed the organizers of the largest meeting that was being held in Kinshasa to include me as their speaker. That trip became very productive. Before we left, we started a program with a local pastor to educate street children that lasted for ten years.

We learnt later when we started the meeting that the bishop who was supposed to be our host, had been arrested by the government for swindling us. I felt sad and asked the government to release him. It would not be good to arrest a man of God despite what he had done to us. I knew God would deal with him. At the same time, I did not want the ministry to be associated with imprisoning anyone, so I requested for his release. They told me the only person who could authorize his release was in the president's office. I called them regarding the matter and told him to escort him to the meeting. Some of the guests did not want him to be released nor to see him at the meeting. I had to demonstrate and live the Word in their presence, 'Do not repay evil with evil'. Indeed, they released him and I let him come to all the meetings but he was very uncomfortable; instead of being our host, the President's office took over to be our host. After we finished, we addressed the issue of dishonesty and he was removed from representing Africa for Jesus Prayer Movement in Kinshasa.

God has been leading this movement and He wants me to write this book for everyone to read and hear this mandate. I pray we will not miss God's visitation this time. He has been patient. His grace continues to use the Body of Christ in different areas. This time however, God wants the Body of Christ to unite so that the world will have no choice but to confess that indeed, Jesus is Lord over the affairs of men and that all nations were created by Him. There is a time and season for every activity, this is the time for the Body of Christ to see Philippians 2:9-11 fulfilled.

> *"Therefore, God exalted him to the highest place and gave him the name that is above every name, that at the name of Jesus every knee should bow, in heaven and on earth and under the earth, and every tongue acknowledge that Jesus Christ is Lord, to the glory of God the Father."*

CHAPTER EIGHT

NOT ME! NOT ANOTHER REVELATION!

Having read this far, I pray you are now convinced that God still speaks and reveals strategies to His children for specific assignments. God operates in times and seasons. Although the name of this mandate is Africa for Jesus, it means All Nations for Jesus. Africa is the mother of the human race; therefore, the entire world needs to realize and recognize that God is the creator of all things and Jesus is the only name given to men for their salvation and redemption. This is the Kairos moment (the right, critical, opportune moment) for the Body of Christ to unite and spread the love of God throughout every nation and every sphere of influence. It is the opportune moment to do practical acts of kindness to your neighbor in your community and nation. The focus indeed is for

Africans, where ever they are, to take the lead to bring end-time revival as it has been prophesied over the years.

In this Kairos moment, God is reminding nations that Africa has been in the center of His creation story and has been used to mold God's chosen people, the Israelites. In Exodus 3:7-10 God spoke to Moses concerning how He had heard the prayers and the cries of the children of Israel in the land of Egypt;

> *The Lord said, "I have indeed seen the misery of my people in Egypt. I have heard them crying out because of their slave drivers, and I am concerned about their suffering. So, I have come down to rescue them from the hand of the Egyptians and to bring them up out of that land into a good and spacious land, a land flowing with milk and honey...... So now, go! I am sending you to Pharaoh to bring my people the Israelites out of Egypt."*

God told Moses to go and set the people free so that they could go to the land that He would show them. I believe God has heard the prayers of His people, especially Africans in Africa and around the world. He wants Africans to be united in order to bring end-time revival as it has been prophesied. Africa was involved in helping Jesus carry the cross to Golgotha, now Jesus is about to align Africa with God's mandate. Their unity would also eliminate some of the ungodly agendas that hinder them from obtaining all the benefits that God has for them. Although there are many "giants" within and out of Africa which are strong and powerful, I believe in the all-powerful God who has given this strategy. The strong walls that hindered God's people from entering the city of Jericho, as God promised, collapsed because of a seemingly foolish strategy God gave to Joshua. Their obedience to God's instruction brought supernatural miracles (Joshua 6). God is waiting for His children to unite on the third Saturday of every month in order for His Kingdom to be revealed in every sphere of society.

Bishop John Gimanez's Prophesy

From the time we obeyed by mobilizing Christians to unite every third Saturday wherever they reside, many have experienced supernatural intervention in the various nations where they have met. As we take it one step at a time, God continues to reveal other strategies. In 2005, God spoke before pastors, bishops, diplomats, expatriates and businessmen, who met to hear an emergency message from Bishop John Gimenez of the Rock Church in Virginia Beach. This happened because the previous night when he was preaching at the All Churches Millennium Service organized by the I GO Ministries and hosted by the Bethel World Outreach Church in Silver Spring, Bishop Gimenez emphasized how God wants Africans to get ready to bring end-time revival to America and around the nations. When Dr. Johnson, the host pastor, heard that message, he announced to the church leaders who were present to return for an emergency meeting the following day. He said, "I know for some of you Monday is your day off, but please come let us meet in the conference room tomorrow morning to hear more of what God is saying to us, especially African leaders."

The following morning, we met in the conference room and Bishop Gimenez shared what God had said about Africa. After that, we started praying for God's revelation about what we had heard. We prayed for a long time and then it was quiet, each of us was still in an attitude of prayer. All of a sudden, as if someone told them to all speak at the same time, in one accord and almost in one voice they said, "In two years' time, something will be done," then they all paused looking at one another. Then one person echoed, "Yes in two years' time!" I also heard in my spirit that something would happen in two years' time. Then we started wondering what would happen. As we discussed, no one heard or knew what would be done or what would happen. No one seemed to have a clear answer. Then they together said again, "Dr. Mordi, you are the one who carries this vision of united prayers for Africa, you are the one who gathered us last night to hear Bishop Gimenez, tell us what God wants done in two years' time."

Being Chosen by God vs Men

As soon as they called my name I protested, "No, bishops and all you leaders! You cannot ask me to do this, it is not for me. God gave me the dates until next year which is 2006. He did not say anything about 2007, that is not for me to say." None of the leaders in that conference room wanted to hear what I was saying. But I kept protesting and said, "You are pastors with churches, God wants you to hear what He is saying for 2007 so you can tell your members." But they did not pay attention to anything I was saying. As they continued to ask me to do it, my emotions got the best of me and with tears I told them how hard it had been to organize the meetings without a proper office, staff or income, having to do everything by faith and depending on volunteers. I went on to tell them that I know God gave me passion to unite the Body of Christ, but after 2006 it was up to them and their church leaders to run with it; they had congregations and prayer ministries who could easily be in charge.

My pastor, Bishop Johnson saw that I was not willing to accept what they were saying. He calmly looked at me and said to them, "Excuse us, let me talk to Dr. Mordi alone outside." He called me outside and said, "Dr. Mordi, don't you see the importance of being chosen? Of all these bishops and business leaders, no one has objected except to ask you to seek God on what He wants us to do? We haven't voted! Yet we all agree for you to lead us." Then he continued, "Nicku do not embarrass your pastor, tell them you will accept and we will help you accomplish what God wants us to do in 2007."

Bishop Johnson is my pastor and a friend, we met at the Oral Roberts University in 1980; I did not want to embarrass nor disrespect him. So, I listened to him and wiped away my tears. We went back inside, and I sat down without smiling. Then he told them that in order for me to effectively do what God wants us to do, he (Bishop Johnson) would allow me to use my office at the church for the AFJ preparations in addition to what I was already doing. However, he requested that each church present make a monthly contribution to pay for a part time staff to help with the assignment. When they started discussing, I excused myself and left the meeting to go home. My heart was heavy and tears rolled down my checks as I pulled out of the parking lot.

Having My Pity-party!

You might be asking why I was so moody and unhappy knowing all the leaders appointed me without any hesitation. Yes, it was an honor but it was a heavy responsibility. I had done it for eleven years, running up and down convincing church leaders to spread the Third Saturday Prayer Strategy and appoint representatives in their congregations for effective implementation of God's mandate, but many did not do it. Imagine, from the time

God gave the dates from 1994 to 2006, we faithfully united the Body of Christ as He had commanded. We had only one year left to complete the assignment on the final date written with His finger on my bedroom wall. Why should I be told that 2007 was also part of God's assignment for me? It did not make sense to me and many questions went through my mind. "Why didn't He include that year when He wrote those other years? Was He out of space? What was going on?" These frustrating thoughts were mixed with emotions of not understanding what God wanted me to do. Why did those leaders select me and not another one amongst themselves? They had church members who would be willing to serve them; they all had salaries and I believed they could easily handle one year.

I had a pity party all by myself as I drove home. When I reached home, I told my husband about how unfair they all were to me. Of course, my complaining and frustration did not make him feel sorry for me, instead he said, "Nicku, that is what you are called to do and God has given you grace to do it." He was no help, I left him alone and rushed to the bedroom to think some more — not spiritual thoughts. I was thinking and hoping that God would tell me not to do anything since I had been faithful in the assignment He gave me in 1994. Now it was 2005, all the team leaders, including myself knew that December 2006 was the end of what was written by the finger of God. How could anyone say otherwise. My thoughts convinced me, "the leaders were mistaken like Priest Eli mistook Hannah of being drunk."

"As she kept on praying to the Lord, Eli observed her mouth. ¹³ Hannah was praying in her heart, and her lips were moving but her voice was not heard. Eli thought she was drunk ¹⁴ and said to her, "How long are you going to stay drunk? Put away your wine."
(1 Samuel 1:12-14)

God speaks concerning 2007

I must have fallen asleep because around 3 am, I was awakened by an unexplainable but refreshing feeling mixed with unnatural joy filled with encouragement from God. He spoke as a Father speaks to a discouraged daughter; He spoke so clearly of what He wanted done in July 2007. My spirit was uplifted and peace came into my spirit, soul and body. I became joyful and excited for the morning to come so I could call Bishop Johnson and tell him what God had done. I don't think I slept for the rest of the night, nor do I remember praying any long prayers. I thanked God over and over for giving me peace and speaking to me unexpectedly. Another thing I remember was looking at the clock several times waiting for day break. By seven o'clock in the morning, I got up and wanted to call Bishop immediately. However, I restrained myself knowing it was too early. I anxiously wanted time to go faster because I could not wait to tell him how God had spoken and ministered to me regarding their request.

It was around 8.30 am — although it was not a time I usually would call Bishop Johnson, I considered urgent, I did not mind making the call that early. Besides, at that time of the morning, I was sure he would not pick up. I intended to leave an urgent message in the answering machine for him to call me back. Indeed, it is good to be in tune with the Spirit of God who is available to lead us in all that we do. Saints, every day the Holy Spirit is available to guide and instruct us, use Him. That morning I dialed his number and on the first ring he picked up the phone. I apologized and said, "Bishop, what you wanted me to hear about 2007, God has revealed to me and I have a message to share with you. What time are you going to the office today?" I did not wait to hear his response, then I continued, "Please come first thing to the office, I will share what you all wanted me to hear from God concerning 2007." I do not remember if he said anything, but I know I hung up the phone feeling very good because I spoke with him and I knew he would also be eager to hear what I had to say. I immediately got ready to go to meet him at the office.

The Church office normally opened at 10:00 am but that day I arrived very early. I sat in my office eagerly waiting for Bishop Johnson to arrive. By 10:15 am, I was impatient and wanted to call and ask where he was. I rushed to see if it was him each time the door opened. I kept walking to look through the outside widow to see if his car had pulled up. I had no patience because of the weight of the task that laid ahead and the fact that God had spoken so quickly. By 10:30 am, I finally saw him coming up the stairs, I rushed to meet him and when he saw me, he asked, "Dr. Mordi, what is so urgent that it could not wait? 2007 is two years away but you rushed me to come." I answered, "Sorry Bishop but this is very important, you remember what happened yesterday? Please come to my office so we can talk!" "Oooh Dr. Mordi, give me few minutes to put my things in my office then I will come," He responded.

I did not even want him to go in his office just in case something interrupted and delay him. But I said, "Okay!" and waited outside his office. I stood there until he came out, then I rushed and opened my office door. As soon as he entered, I closed the door behind him. And before I sat down, I began telling him, "Bishop, that was God who made you pick up the phone this morning because of what happened in the meeting yesterday. You all felt God was saying in two years' time, Africa get ready! You all asked me to seek God on what He wanted us to do next. You saw how I did not want to do it but you encouraged me to listen to the desire of the leaders. I left with a heavy heart and I drove back home very upset. I thought God was not going to talk to me because I had no desire to hear from Him. When I mentioned to my husband what you all wanted me to do and how I refused to hear, my husband was not sympathetic so I went to my bedroom to continue my pity part." All this time, as I was talking, Bishop just sat there listening. I went on, "I don't remember if I fell asleep but I felt God's peace and encouragement inside me, I was not upset or distraught anymore."

God Requires Praises in Nations

As peace flooded my entire being, then I heard God say these words: "In 2007, mobilize Christians in every nation for a praise and thanksgiving rally on the third Saturday of July, use the same dates as before. You have prayed for the nations, now hold rallies and offer thanksgiving prayers as you wave the flag to demonstrate your unity and declare my purpose for the nations." While God was saying those words, unexplainable peace continued to flood my mind and soul. At that moment, I felt I could handle all He was telling me to do. It sounded so simple and easy. Then God concluded with, 'let praises go forth all over the nations.' Then His presence left the room."

I continued to tell Bishop Johnson with excitement, "All the bishops, pastors, ambassadors and expatriates who came to the conference room yesterday, must be called and told what God has said we should do in

2007." Bishop could see how excited I was as I shared my encounter with God as opposed to the previous day when the Church Leaders were talking to me. I was distraught and did not want to do what they were asking of me. But after I heard from God, everything changed. When you hear from the Creator, you do not remain the same, you are empowered to believe that nothing is impossible. After I finished sharing with him, bishop immediately said, "That is great Dr. Mordi, let us call an emergency meeting. Tell them we can meet in my office tomorrow." Immediately I responded, "No, I cannot call them, you are the Chairman and they will be coming to your office, it would be better if you called them to come back tomorrow, Wednesday, January 12, 2005."

Bishop's Emergency Meeting

My reason for refusing to call was because on Sunday evening, we had All Churches Prayer Service that I GO hosted every year to unite the Body of Christ. The following Monday, a few of them returned to hear Bishop Gimenez's message for African Churches, then Tuesday was when I was sharing the encounter I had had with God. I felt they would not come again on Wednesday if I called them unless Bishop Johnson himself called them to return.

Indeed, he made the calls and on Wednesday, the I GO Africa for Jesus Executive Board and other leaders who were in the Monday morning meeting came. I told them God wanted the Church Body to hold thanksgiving prayers and praise in every African country and all over the world where Africans and Friends of Africa reside. We should also start encouraging Africans for political positions in the United States and work with ambassadors to identify nationals who like politics. Then in 2006 hold a Thanksgiving Rally at the Washington Mall to showcase the bilateral contributions of Africans in the USA before the 2007 mandate. The entire leadership team including some Christian African Ambassadors were on board and we started to prepare what we called "2007 Continental Prayer and Thanksgiving Praise Campaign."

The July 2006 rally to gather Africans in the Diaspora from across the world to the nation's capital was a great strategy because it helped to promote the 2007 Continental Prayer and Thanksgiving Praise Campaign to be held all over the world. The Bethel Church in Silver Spring became the center for the 2006 Rally in Washington, DC as well as the preparation for the 2007 Continental Prayer and Thanksgiving Campaign.

Gods Thoughts are Not our Thoughts!

These experiences, cemented in my heart the truth that God does not do anything except what He has revealed to His prophets. Although He always wants to talk to His children and guide them to do what He wants them to do, often times we miss the opportunity because we are operating on a different frequency, we do not produce what God intends and we become victims of circumstances. When we hear from Him, we make the mistake of doing what is convenient for us or what we are accustomed to doing. In most cases, we desire to disobey rather than to inconvenience ourselves especially if He tells us to do things that are unfamiliar. But God's thoughts are not our thoughts, neither our ways, His ways — God is God (Jer. 55:8). Also we forget what the scripture says,

> *"What no eye has seen, what no ear has heard, and what no human mind has conceived the things God has prepared for those who love him."* (I Corinthians 2:9)

I thank God for those who always go an extra mile to advance His Kingdom by their continuous dependence on what the Holy Spirit directs them to do. God's Kingdom agenda is greater than any one institution. Uniting our efforts for a specific cause will help the Church accomplish much more to fulfill the Great Commission and to bring God's Kingdom to earth as it is in heaven.

Unfortunately, the July 2006 mandate to be done at the D.C. Mall did not happen. No one had heard or seen a thanksgiving rally done by Africans that unites different nations, denominations and politicians, it was hard to embrace the idea. That is another reason the 2006 rally that was supposed to take place at the D.C. Mall did not take place. Also, I was not aware that large projects like that needed sponsors and great publicity to make it succeed. Instead, we met at Bishop Owen's Church on Rhode Island Avenue, N.E., Washington, DC. Since we did not do exactly as God had instructed, we missed the opportunity to impact society with God's righteousness, especially the Washington Metropolitan area.

You are aware that many ungodly agendas can take place when God's instruction or natural law is not followed properly. Let's try to have a balance, to not be more concerned with building our own kingdoms at the expense of God's Kingdom Agenda. Indeed, it is good to do well with what He has called you to do, it is God who gave different gifts, vision, dreams and the different responsibilities as the Word clearly say,

> *"So Christ himself gave the apostles, the prophets, the evangelists, the pastors and teachers, to **equip his people** for works of service, so that the body of Christ may be built up until we all reach unity in the faith and in the knowledge of the Son of God **and become mature**, attaining to the whole measure of the fullness of Christ." (Ephesians 4:11-13)*

However, it is the same God who has instructed us to once a while; when He has a specific purpose to benefit the larger picture of building His Kingdom, all these different talents, gifts, ministries, visions and dreams unite for the sole purpose of giving Him praise and thanksgiving. When we are thankful, God would do what He alone can do

This revelation about God writing actual dates on the wall of my bedroom is unnatural and it is taking many years to be understood. How He gave the mandate for Christians to unite as One Body to pray for Africa and other nations on those specific dates leaves no doubt that it is a divine assignment. The different activities that He guides to be done in July in several countries has a progression like the vision Ezekiel was given of how the water started from his ankles, then the water went to his knees then it reached his loins until it became a big river that could not be passed over (Ezek. 47:3-5).

This is the time and season for Christians to unite and become a bigger army for end-time revival. By writing specific dates did not mean we should not pray for nations at other times. He was only instructing us to be in one accord on that specific day; speaking as one Body regarding God's will on earth. We can pray for twenty-four hours throughout the year, but there comes a time when unity of purpose is necessary, especially when God takes the trouble to write down the instructions in order to avoid any misunderstanding. He is God who does what He wills.

Not My Will but God's Will

Indeed, we have seen the amazing Hand of God and His wisdom guiding us every step of the way. I pray you'd agree that the Third Saturday mandate is one of God's Strategy for end-time impact. Many people have not heard about it. Some have not embraced it because they think it is a personal ministry and they have their own ministries. I have spent time to lay a foundation on how this Prayer Movement began and the importance of following God's instructions even if we are not sure of what He is saying. It is my hope that the Holy Spirit is speaking with you or will speak to you as you come to the understanding of the Biblical meaning and importance of the Third Day revelation in scriptures.

For emphasis, let me reiterate, as you have read above and you continue to read, I pray you would realize that this is not something that I birthed but this is what the Holy Spirit instructed me to share with the Body of Christ. I am just His workman carrying this end-time strategy to the Church Body anywhere around the world. I have often wanted to give up, but God always shows up to encourage me with supernatural signs. For example, one night at around 3 am, God stopped me from praying and ordered me to go and watch television. It didn't sound spiritual at all; it felt like an instruction from the devil himself and I rebuked him seriously. "How can I stop praying to watch television?" But I was mistaken, it was God wanting to show me what was taking place in Zambia, Africa. Afterward, I had to repent for mistaking His voice.

I mentioned how two doves refused to fly in Israel in Chapter One; over 300 people witnessed seven doves released on the open colosseum but two did not fly no matter how hard they tried, they remained on the podium. At night those two doves showed up at my bedroom window carrying the Praying for Africa Christian Unity Flag and the sign that said, "WORD". God told me why they did not fly for all to see, then He gave me specific instructions connected to the Third Saturday unity. Rehashing what He said, "They fulfilled their agenda but not My mandate, and that is why I could not let the doves fly. However, My grace is still upon the church to fulfill My kingdom agenda; that is why five of the doves flew away."

It is an awesome responsibility to deliver prophetic message. Obeying God has always been a priority even in very hard situations. I have tried to encourage the Church around different parts of the world to engage in Unity Prayer, thank God slow change is manifesting although some people continue in their programs without having the burden to unite. As I was getting weary of trying to share the mandate, another supernatural sign took place. The 2016 East Coast snowstorm printed the continent of Africa including the island of Madagascar on my front lawn. Then God, using the image of Africa on the snow, revealed many things in the same context as what He said in Israel, at the Bill Graham Ridgecrest center in North Carolina and what He had been saying on several occasions. Many more supernatural miracles and phenomena would be written in another book titled, "Blind Faith II: 20th Century Phenomenon."

God has, from when we began in 1994, been expanding this mandate with specific purpose for each country. This is not for Africa or Africans alone, although that is what He started with, this is for all who believe in the return of Jesus. It is appropriate to say that the Third Saturday Unity Prayer is for the entire Body of Christ around the world. As you continue to read the rest of the chapters and study the Word of God for yourself you will realize, even more the importance of the Third Day in scriptures. I pray you will automatically desire to follow the Word and the end-time strategy that God wrote down with His finger on my bedroom wall. It is no longer mine alone to carry but His entire Body.

The entire experience is hard to precisely put in words; no one can articulate or explain divine encounters except to depend on the Holy Spirit to make it clear. I have no doubt that God uses numeric codes to show authenticity. It is God who made sure there is a perfect mathematical design in time and space. God speaks through numbers, parables, type and symbols to conceal what He is saying.

Proverb 25:2 says, *"It is the glory of God to conceal a matter; to search out a matter is the glory of kings.* I believe God ended at 2006 because number six is a number of men and He added the year 2007 for the Church leaders who met in Silver Spring because seven is a spiritual number of completion. I am convinced God was telling the entire Body of Christ that we are in the last days and it is a new season for us to complete the job of the Great Commission. It is up to the Church Leaders to prepare the Body of Christ for end-time impact.

Mandated to be Thankful

It is unbelievable how the entire movement has been led by following numbers in accordance with spiritual meaning. Once again, if in 2008 God spoke about enhancing the prayer strategy by having Thanksgiving rallies across the nations would have been because number eight is a number of new beginnings. In spite of praying without ceasing, God wants His children to be filled with gratitude for all that He has done and what He is about to do. In the Old Testament, some Levites were appointed to give continuous praise and thanksgiving to God as written in 1 Chronicles 16:8 – 9; *'Give praise to the LORD, PROCLAIM HIS NAME, MAKE KNOWN AMONG THE NATIONS WHAT HE HAS DONE. Sing to him, sing praise to him; tell of all his wonderful acts.* He also required them as individuals to give thanksgiving to the Lord not empty handed, but by waving sacrificial offering.

"Say to the Israelites: 'Anyone who brings a fellowship offering to the Lord is to bring part of it as their sacrifice to the Lord. ³⁰ With their own hands they are to present the food offering to the Lord; they are to bring the fat, together with the breast, and wave the breast before the Lord as a wave offering."
(Leviticus 7:28-30)

How much more Christians in the New covenant, we should be the most thankful people who don't take God's grace for granted. Indeed, it is the only religion in the world that worships the resurrected Lord Jesus Christ who is the ultimate fulfillment of all that the Old Testament sacrifices. His death on the cross was the perfect sacrifice for all our sins to be completely forgiven. Jesus Christ did not remain in the grave, but on the third Day He became alive so that we can live also.

The resurrection is a reminder to those who study the Word of God as a historical document only; they go to church as if they are going to a memorial service. Our Lord Jesus is not among the dead. He lives! He reigns in the hearts of those who have surrendered their lives to Him. Jesus is the Head of His Church and He rose on the Third Day; He lives and loves us with unconditional love. Christians have to be convinced of the resurrection power that is within them to live victorious lives without compromise by embracing the Third Day resurrection power to enable you to say,

"Who shall separate us from the love of Christ? Shall trouble or hardship or persecution or famine or nakedness or danger or sword? ... No, in all these things we are more than conquerors through him who loved us. ³⁸ For I am convinced that neither death nor life, neither angels nor demons, neither the present nor the future, nor any powers, ³⁹ neither height nor depth, nor anything else in all creation, will be able to separate us from the love of God that is in Christ Jesus our Lord," (Romans 8:35-39).

Indeed, these are evil days, Christians must be convinced that nothing would be able to separate them from the love of God. It is a new day to take our stand because there is all indication that God is moving us towards the final preparation of the return of His Son, Jesus Christ. This Third Day Mystery may give us some breakthrough strategies to foster our unity for His return. This is a wake-up call for every individual to use their gifts and talent to accomplish the Great Commission anywhere they are before He returns.

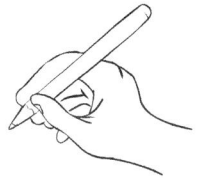

CHAPTER NINE

THE THIRD DAY MYSTERY

Through years of praying on the Third Saturday of every month I started studying about the significance of the number three in scripture. When I urged people to unite on the Third Day or Third Saturday, they often said the day did not matter as long as they were praying for the nations. Yes, and I pray for nations every day of the week. Many churches and ministries have prayer meetings and people do pray for nations all the time. I can emphatically say there is no day that people do not pray. However, ask yourself this question, "If God gives you an instruction, what will you do?" I believe you should try to obey what you are told, otherwise God would question whether you are serious. This is what happened to me, the Third Saturday was not originated by me but by God Himself. He revealed it to me like He revealed the deep and hidden things to David and to several others in the scriptures (Daniel 2:22, 1 Cor. 2:19).

When you do not know what God is saying through symbolism with certain numbers, you would miss what God is saying altogether. On my own, I could not handle anything, I had to seek God for His wisdom and spiritual understanding to the deep meaning of those revelations. It took a few years before He answered me through His Word. I was excited and surprised that I did not understand Him sooner because there is no work or word without number. Nevertheless, I am filled with gratitude that He chose me to be a mouthpiece for what might bring practical and effortless end-time unity. I invite you to explore with me a few examples from the Word of God which has empowered me to be absolutely certain that this might be one of the end-time strategies for God's Kingdom to be more visible in societies and in nations.

The Number Three

The **number three** or its compounds occur hundreds of times in scripture. Most of them simply refer to quantity whether it is persons, things, or activities. For example:

◆ Noah had **three sons** (Gen 6:10).

◆ Job had **three daughters** (Job 1:2; cf. 42:13).

- The Ark of the Covenant contained **three sacred objects:** 'The gold jar of manna, Aaron's staff that had budded, and the stone tablets of the covenant" (Heb. 9:4).

- Daniel prayed **three times** a day (Dan. 6:10-13).

- Men of Israel from 13 years of age were supposed to appear **three times** before the Lord.

- Also, we often speak in **threes:** such as talking about a day, a month or a year. Summer, winter or spring. Also, Angels cry Holy, Holy, Holy etc.

The Third Day

As you study the Word, you will find that there are references made to the **Third Day.** It is usually a day or a time which something of significance takes place. The **Third Day** also indicates a designated period of waiting, followed by an expected decision or activity such as waiting for a special spiritual event.

The book of Hosea has stylistic literary pattern of the concept of the number three. Bible writers, inspired by the Holy Spirit, often presented things in a "threefold" way with special emphasis on completeness or indicating anticipation of further ramifications of what has been spoken or shown. God's design to reveal special events to His creation. The **"Third Day"** seems to provide a rhetorical pattern to prepare and alert those familiar with God's revelation. This is true regarding the resurrection of Jesus Christ. The **Third Day** ensures a complete act of redemption as well as an expectation of more to follow.

Moreover, the **Third Day** Resurrection of Christ gives confidence to believers that they should consciously live and depend on the resurrection power to help them in this life's journey. Because Jesus rose from the dead, He has now taken residence in the lives of Christians. Galatians 2:20 says,

> *"I have been crucified with Christ and I no longer live, but Christ lives in me. The life I now live in the body, I live by faith in the Son of God, who loved me and gave himself for me."*

Through His resurrection we know that He is helping us to genuinely live a Godly and holy life (Col. 3:1-40). The Bible further says: *"...but we have one who has been tempted in every way, just as we are yet was without sin"* (Heb. 4:15).

When we obey the Word of God, we are renewed and our lives are victorious and steadfast despite all the problems we face. Keep in mind that Jesus faced all kinds of troubles and was betrayed by His own, but His dependence on the Word of God allowed Him to live a victorious life. When He was in the desert, He overcame the **threefold** temptation from Satan by quoting **three scriptures** (Matt. 4:1-11). Note how the **number three** is applied in different passages of Scriptures. As you follow these patterns, pray you will understand why it is imperative for Christians to unite where ever they are on the **Third Saturday of every month.** This is the season to adjust our regular activities to include this end-time strategy that does not cost anything.

Three Months

A three-month period in scriptures also has special significance which demonstrates important action or events that took place in the history of God's people. Here are a few examples: When the Egyptian Pharaoh enslaved the Hebrews because he was afraid that they were becoming too strong as they increased in number; he was afraid they might threaten his leadership and overthrow him. He gave a decree to kill all the male children born to Hebrew women. However, there was a clever mother who refused to obey the decree of the king, Jochebed Amram hid her son for **three months** and became the first mother to design a floating basket that she put on the Nile river. The basket was made of papyrus reeds and tar, which made it waterproof (Exodus. 2:2-3). Through the divine orchestration of God, the young boy was taken by Pharaoh's daughter who named him 'Moses'. She raised him in the home of the same king who killed all other male Hebrew boys.

Obey God's word, Despite

Indeed, God will protect your destiny regardless of what the enemy would try to do. Moses' life was nurtured by the enemy of his people — God's ways are not your ways nor His plans, your plans. He envisions a future bigger and better than you could ever imagine; just obey and do what He tells you to do.

> *"For I know the plans I have for you," declares the Lord, "plans to prosper you and not to harm you, plans to give you hope and a future. Then you will call on me and come and pray to me, and I will listen to you. You will seek me and find me when you seek me with all your heart. I will be found by you," (Jeremiah 29:11-14a)*

As a child of God, when you are faced with unavoidable challenges or evil, look for ways to do something, never give up and never do nothing about it. Your courage and determination to take action will cause God to raise even your enemy to help you like He did with Moses.

Another example of why it is vital to obey God's instructions even if it does not make sense to you, is given in the following Biblical examples. This sad example is about a man of God who was killed by God for doing what was right and noble in the eyes of the people. Uzzah and Ahio guarded the Ark of the Covenant when it was being transferred by oxen (cows) from the house of Aminadab to Jerusalem. As they travelled, the ox stumbled and the

Ark on the back was about to fall off the cart. Uzzah stretched forth his hand to steady the ark so that it would not fall, it was an automatic reaction that anyone could have taken. In fact, it was a noble thing to protect God's Ark from falling but he was struck dead immediately for doing what seemed right to him and to others. Indeed, God's ways are not our ways.

> *"When they came to the threshing floor of Kidon, Uzzah reached out his hand to steady the ark, because the oxen stumbled. ¹⁰ The Lord's anger burned against Uzzah, and he struck him down because he had put his hand on the ark. So he died there before God",* *(1 Chron. 13:9-10).*

As a result of this incident, the people became afraid and refused to continue. For **three months**, the Ark of the Covenant stayed in the house of Obed-Edom instead of being taken on to Jerusalem (1 Chronicles 13:14).

This is one of the reasons I continue to talk about the **Third Saturday unity**. If God took time to write it all out on the wall of my bedroom, and those numbers are still important to this day, it only makes sense for the Body of Christ to heed His instructions. Uzzah died because he did not follow the instruction God had given on how the ark should be carried (Numbers 4:5-15). The Ark was Holy and consecrated and was not to be touched by human hands. Although he was sincere in trying to prevent the ark from falling, he had to face the consequences of not following God's instructions. **We must understand, obedience to God's laws or instructions are more important than our programs or agendas of doing good things.** This is so important!

This also shows the **three-edged manifestation** of God. He is **perfect loving, just, and all-powerful**. It is an undeniable fact that blessings come to those who obey Him and punishment goes to those who disobey or disregard His instructions. The punishment might come swiftly or over a time, but it will come.

Imagine Young Mary

Thank God for His grace and His longsuffering as we fall short of comprehending His Word, especially when revealed in an uncommon manner. As we continue to look into His Word concerning the significance of the **number three**, there is still so much that I have not covered. The New Testament talks about the angel Gabriel, who was sent to visit a young virgin called Mary. Can you imagine? She was in a small village minding her own business when God sent an envoy to her. Never give up, your time will come when God will surprise you with a visitation from heaven. He might frighten you by giving you an assignment or say something that is beyond your ability or beyond the norm, do not fear because you are created to do great things, it is in your DNA. Personally,

I have been faced with divine fear several times and it is hard to explain to others unless they have had divine encounters.

The Virgin Mary was told that she would conceive a son by the Holy Spirit. That was beyond impossible; it was crazy and unheard of. She was too young to even fully understand what was happening. When she tried to tell the others, no one understood her or paid any close attention to what she was saying. I can assume she was ignored and dismissed or even rebuked for saying such an impossible thing. They might have called her all kinds of names as being a crazy young girl who was hallucinating or having a fantasy of being impregnated by an angel. Even her fiancé Joseph did not want to hear such news, what I call the "Unprecedented Biblical Scandal." Mary was frustrated and could not handle what was happening to her. She had to go to a mature woman of God to share her fears and her experience of being pregnant without knowing a man in order to be guided further. Her visit to Elizabeth lasted for **three months** (Lk 1:56). I pray you begin to understand this revelation of why the number, **three is** associated with important events in the Word of God.

Imagine Paul's Suffering

When Paul started to preach, he stayed in Ephesus and in Greece, spending **three months** in each place (Acts 19:8; 20:3). Some unfortunate things happened to him after **three months**. When Paul was being taken as a prisoner to Rome, the ship was wrecked **three times** and they had to stay in Malta for **three months** (Acts 28:11). In the midst of difficulties, Paul did not stop doing what he was called to do. Knowing he was a prisoner who was unfairly accused, he continued to preach the Gospel which transformed many leaders in Malta. For the **three months** they waited for the ship to be repaired in order to continue the journey, Paul did not feel sorry for himself. Instead, he became more enthusiastic about spreading the Good News of God's love and grace through Jesus Christ.

No matter what situation you find yourself in. No matter how unfairly you are being treated, do not focus on yourself, focus on the big picture of God's love that is so personal. Focus on how He sent Jesus to redeem and save you as an individual. Even those who may treat you unfairly, are to be a part of His Kingdom; Focus on the bigger picture of being called to serve in the mission to honor the King of kings. If you train to do that in every situation, you would be steadfast and unmovable. Remember your challenges are part of life. *Everything works out for good to them that love God and are the called according to His purpose* (Romans 8:28).

When the Word says that everything or "all things" work together for our good, it does not mean that all that happens to us is good. Evil is prevalent everywhere, especially in these days of advanced technology and freedom of speech; people harm others without any reason. But God has all power to turn these evil circumstances for His glory if we would focus on Him and not on ourselves. Those who are called by His name have a different perspective, their minds have been transformed to accept with gratitude whatever life brings that is beyond their control. Above all, everything will work for their good because their mindset about their experiences of pain, persecution or hardship does not cause resentment because they know God is with them and His grace is sufficient.

Three Years

Briefly, we have looked at Biblical references of the number **three, Third Day** and **the third month.** Now, let's conclude with events that have **Three Years' Significance.** These incidents were significant in the lives of the children of Israel when they entered the promised land. Keep in mind what was stated earlier, that God does not do anything without revealing it to His prophets (Amos 3:7.), or as I often say, *"God reveals things to His children who have an intimate relationship with Him, who love to communicate with Him, who have the revelatory understanding of who they are in Him and to Him."*

This is my personal experience with my Heavenly Father. Several examples above show He knows my desire to be intimate with Him. How he entered my bedroom that night and how His hand appeared to write down dates on my bedroom wall, then instructed me to copy because He knew I could forget the instruction for His Body so He took His time to write and watch me copy them. I believe if I had awakened that morning and found those numbers on the kitchen table, I would have probably ignored them, or I wouldn't have noticed them at all. But since He took time to wake me up and write while He watched me copy, He meant business and we had to be serious as well. What He did was not for show, but it was an important assignment that He knew I was not about to accept willingly. Moreover, the assignment was for Church leaders for His children all over the world.

Cultivate an Intense Desire to Walk with God

My intense desire to know Him better, walk closer with Him, and to obey Him in all things that started when I was a young girl has helped me to avoid unnecessary self-inflicting wounds that has afflicted others. I decided a long time ago to obey and do God's will when Jesus appeared on a motor-cycle in my small village of Isanga in Mbeya, Tanzania. As I was washing dirty cooking pots outside our home, He stopped His motor-cycle and said, "Come, ride with me." I did not rise immediately because I was not finished with what I was doing. He insisted seriously that I follow Him, as I hesitated, He started to leave. Immediately, I left everything and hopped on the motorcycle behind Him as dirty as I was. Something within me could not allow me to let Him go. As He drove, we reached a place called Ilomba, it was filled with people of all sizes and colors, then He said to me, "Feel at home." That is the life I was called live and it is a life I have chosen to follow and I have been riding with Him until today.

That night I realized what was happening was not a dream nor a vision but a reality. God's presence through His Holy Spirit was there writing the numbers on my wall. Because I did not understand it at the time, I kept on questioning what was happening, anticipating that the revelation would be explained for me to totally understand but that did not happen. I had to take a step of faith and share what I was told rather than keep quiet. Although the entire team did not understand the incredible revelation, by faith we took action by setting up meetings on the **Third Saturday** as explained in the earlier chapters. After a year or so we realized the dates that were written were all on the **Third Saturday of every month**. Since then *God has continued to reveal precept upon precept*. The message is the same and the day is the same but different strategies of what to do and how to do it continues to be revealed.

Here are more biblical examples pertaining to **Third Year**. In the Old Testament, as part of the Levitical stipulations referencing the year of Jubilee, the Hebrews were not allowed to farm, sow or reap on the 15th year. In compensation, God promised to send blessings in the 16th year that the land would yield enough to last them **for three years** (Lev. 25:21). In another example, Absalom, the son of King David, after killing his brother, fled to Geshur and stayed there **for three years** (2 Sam. 13:38). The story of when God told Prophet Isaiah to go barefoot for **three years** (Isa. 20:3-4) as a sign of protest against Egypt and Cush, is very interesting.

I believe this is another reason God instructed us to use Africa for Jesus, because He has heard the prayers of His people, the shame and anger He had against these people have been paid for. Jesus was stripped naked and went barefoot to redeem us. It is a new day for His children not to continue living in the sins of the past but to unite and make declarations to bring God's kingdom to every sphere of society. Like the wisest man who ever lived, King Solomon, said, *there is a time and a season for every action under the heaven.* We must know that this is the time for embracing the significance of the end-time Kingdom strategy. Notice, even Apostle Paul spent **three years** in the desert to seek and commune with God in order to prepare for God's Kingdom agenda (Gal. 1:18).

In light of the examples mentioned above, note that a great many things happened when the number **three** was mentioned, **be it three days, three months, or three years.** This is more than mere coincidence. There is too much evidence to think "**three**" is an ordinary number. God was very intentional then, and I believe He is very intentional now. He has a divine purpose that He has continued to address for over 26 years now. There are divine phenomena that have taken place and have been witnessed by those who are familiar with the Africa for Jesus Prayer Movement or the **Third Saturday united prayers.** Those supernatural miracles are topics for another book.

The economy of nations also, depend on the obedience of God's people. As mentioned early on regarding the **Third Day** resurrection in the Prophecy of Hosea, there are other incidents mentioned which were not only important for the **economy** of Israel, but also were significant to God's blessings: grain, new wine and oil (Hosea 2:22; 14: 5-07; Joel 1:10; 2:18-19) to name a few. In fact, the first time the **Third Day** appears in the Word of God is in relation to productivity; what the ground produced and continues to produce.

"The land produced vegetation, plants bearing seed according to their kind and trees bearing fruits with seed in it according to their kind. And God saw that

*it was good. And there was evening and there was morning the **THIRD DAY**..."* (Genesis 1:12-13)

When you meet on the Third day for united prayers, you can declare productivity in nations to reduce hunger and improve the productivity of any good enterprise. There is still too much evil that continues to abound in spite of the many prayers that are going forth everywhere. God is ready to do what only He can do if the Body of Christ would align with what He has commanded and continues to reveal. He understands our diversity, yet He commands us to unite once a month for a Kingdom agenda. This is an easy assignment because it does not require any sacrifices except to obey and purpose in your minds to unite with others to make declarations concerning His will and purpose for your area.

Number **Three** also carries with it accompanying implications or expectations. It can signify completeness or finality: **Father, Son and Holy Spirit.** It also brings expectations of further development or supernatural action to follow. Indeed, **three** is an evocative number filled with connotations of special importance that carries additional meaning or nuances because when God spoke to those who later heard or read of the **Third Day** incidents, they were familiar with possible outcomes in their choices. The same applies to present-day prophetic instructions that have been given concerning the **Third Day Unity** of the Body of Christ to pray and make declarations for the transformation of families, communities societies and nations. It is a sign that the Great Commission is being fulfilled. God is ready to intervene as we speak and act as One Body — If we are one, then the world would believe!

CHAPTER TEN

THIRD DAY PRACTICAL ANALYSIS

I n some Biblical contexts, the **Third Day** presents new information that call for further action. Ask yourselves some questions as you read what took place on these particular third days.

♦ On the **Third Day,** Laban found out that Jacob had fled with both wives and properties (Gen 31:22). That is strange! Why not find out on the 2nd day?

♦ Also, on the **Third Day**, Joshua learned that the Gibeonites used deception to sign a treaty of peace with Israel (1 Sam. 29:1-11).

At other times, the decision to be reached on the **Third day** preceded spiritual preparation.

- Queen Esther instructed her uncle, Mordecai, to fast for **three days** before she approached the King of Persia (Esther 4:15-16).

- On the **Third Day**, Esther put on her Royal robe and approached the King (Esther 5:1). This is our time to approach our King without any fear.

- Abraham left without any idea where he was going except to obey God, but on the **Third Day** when he lifted up his head, he knew he had arrived at a place where God sent him — near Mount Morriah (Gen. 22:4).

- After their purification on Mt. Sinai, on the **Third Day**, God appeared to the Children of Israel and His glory frightened them. God spoke to Moses and gave him a code of conduct which we call the Ten Commandments (Ex. 19:14-20:1-17) during those **three days**.

There is no question that the **THIRD DAY** pointed to distinct spiritual dimensions, physical healing, as well as to political protection, when people followed God's instructions.

- On the **Third Day,** the meat which was left after the sacrifice was to be destroyed (Leviticus 7:17-18; 19:6-9). The day was also to be kept holy.

- On the **Third Day,** God promised that Hezekiah would be healed so that he could go up to the temple of the Lord to pray. God promised to heal and protect the city as well (2 Kings 20: 1-6).

- On the **Third Day,** Hosea prophesied healing and restoration if people would repent and return to the God who forgives (Hosea 6:1-2).

Today, many nations are going through different struggles. Some need restoration from political unrest; some need peace, hope, and healing in their bodies, minds and souls. We have read various scriptural references concerning the **Third Day;** is it possible for supernatural interventions to happen if we obeyed the present **Third Saturday Unity of Thanksgiving Prayer and Praise mandate?** Is it possible if we unite to declare God's will upon communities and nations; God will do what He alone can do! The problems that have been so hard to solve after much money and human ingenuity have been applied; it could be that the answers lie in our obedience to HIM. What seems hard to solve by human efforts can easily be solved by God, *"For nothing is impossible with God"* (Luke 1:36-37).

As you have read, the **Third Day** generated further action which had to be followed by those involved. This is the same requirement for Christians to gather once a month for thanksgiving prayers and to make decrees regarding the prayers that have gone forth. There is a time to pause and give God praise before the manifestation comes. The **Third Day** in the Word of God preceded spiritual preparation in order to receive or to hear God. Indeed, this is what has been happening in our annual gatherings, for three days before the Third Saturday, we conduct teaching seminars in every system of influence and challenge Christians to higher standards of integrity and accountability; to recognize the times and live to fulfill the Great Commission. Friday before the Third Saturday, we focus on repentance and allow God to search us in order to move as we make declarations,

> *"I the Lord search the heart and examine the mind, to reward each person according to their conduct, according to what their deeds deserve." (Jeremiah 17:10)*

As Children of God, we must become effective salt and shining light in the dark world.

CONCLUSION

HELP TO REASON WITH ME

C an you imagine, if church leaders operating in the five-fold ministries around the world took it upon themselves to use the third Saturday of every month to unite and declare with conviction, God's will to be manifested in their communities, to have the understanding that this mandate is not one person's agenda but, an agenda for the entire Body of Christ. Can you imagine what God could do among us?

♦ Could this strategy resurrect all the dead dreams and ideas in the lives of God's people?

♦ Could this Third Saturday Prayer Unity help people to have the revelation of who they are and what they were created to be?

- Could this strategy cause Christians to enter boldly before the King of kings and receive all that Christ accomplished on the cross for them?

- Could this Third Saturday Unity bring national transformation of peace, unity and open the eyes of the next generation to achieve dreams that advance God's kingdom in every sphere of influence?

- Could this Third Saturday Unity of declaration cause righteous leaders to rule nations with integrity? Would it lead leaders to receive God's wisdom on how to lead people?

- Could this Third Saturday Unity uncover the natural resources God deposited in nations for the benefit of God's people?

- Could this Third Saturday Unity usher in our Lord since it is a number of completeness?

I am sure you have other ideas that you could share of what could happen if people obeyed God's instructions and united for a cause that is greater than their own. I really do not have an answer except the knowing that God could not have written the dates down and instructed me to copy them if it was not for the entire Christendom. Do you recall as I mentioned the 1999 panic about the Y2K computer crash? Those around me and all those who were involved in the Third Saturday united Prayers suffered no panic because we were privileged to have received instructions from God that went well beyond the year 2000. However, there were a few who joined the panic because they did not believe what I had seen and shared.

With the **Third Saturday** unity of purpose, the Body of Christ would discover the power that they have been given by God to influence every sphere of society for the transformation of nations. There is no entity on earth that has as much power as the Church, yet her power lies dormant because many in the Body of Christ only focus on the spiritual aspect of the "priestly" and not the "kingly" anointing. Also, the reality of working with only a "part of the body" instead of the "whole Body." Because of this oversight, God wants the **Third Saturday unity** to awaken the church to influence all the systems of power in society: government, education, economy, health, family, religion, art and technology. This is why I am sharing this with conviction to spread this strategy because it works. Tanzania is an example of what united prayers have done. God raised a political leader who has the fear of God. Jehovah can do it in any nation. Arise, Christians and embrace it; God is not mocked!

IMPORTANT NOTICE

Finally, whenever you conduct the third Saturday unity prayers, involve professionals and experts of all those areas of influence to teach and impart knowledge to future generations, as well as equip Christians to realize the power of their assignments. In addition, once a year conduct seminars and conferences before the Thanksgiving prayer and praise rallies, do practical projects to help the needy and transform communities. Consistently walk in unity to impact your community and society for His glory. I have recent examples that have inspired me even more to share this strategy with Christians, especially those who want to reach out and influence others for His glory. God has different strategies for different people and nations.

We must realize that the enemy tries to use all kinds of gimmicks to hinder us from fulfilling what we are created to be and to do. Consider this example in the Word, two disciples who were a part of Jesus' ministry for **Three years** at one point did not recognize him. The disciples were going to Emmaus with heavy hearts and kept wondering what had happened to their master. Jesus met them and started walking and talking with them, but they did not recognize him. They were consumed with grief over the fact that their dreams and hopes had been shattered, how the one person they expected to help them, had been killed. They were concerned because it was the **Third Day** and Jesus was still missing.

Think for a moment of what many of us go through when things bombard our minds and disturb our peace. We sometimes miss to hear the still small voice that says to you, "It will be okay." We tend to pay more attention to the loud voice of our struggles and problems. Although Jesus kept walking and talking with them, they did not recognize Him. One good thing that they did was they compelled the stranger to stay with them. If they had not done that, they would have missed their visitation (Luke 24:13-32)

Can you think of a time when you missed an opportunity because you did not take seriously what you heard or the advice you were given? Maybe you have never experienced it personally, but you know those who have made poor decisions and have later regretted. Some people and ministries are still facing the consequences of their bad choices. I pray my writing these personal encounters with God will inspire any child of God to confidently know that God is alive and He still speak. Be inspired by my own faith struggles with being instructed to speak about the **Third Saturday** unity strategy; and to promote the Christian Unity Flag to be used by all who believe that God's Kingdom would be established on earth as we each use our talents and gifts for His glory.

APPEAL TO LEADERS: I am appealing to leaders to take a step of faith and include this strategy in your churches and ministries, especially these days when Satan's agents are so busy spreading the message of Anti-

Christ and evil continues to be celebrated in our nations and around the world. We cannot sit by passively, but must try to do our best to promote kingdom unity. We therefore, request that Christians in every walk of life, especially Christian leaders, own this mandate and run with it to advance God's Kingdom. God would be well pleased — Psalms 133.

How to Identify the Third Day

I believe you agree that God speaks through numbers, parables, symbols and any other method He chooses. In our context, He took time to write specific dates in a 12-year interval that fell on the third Saturday of each month, this is why we call it the **Third Saturday United Prayers of Thanksgiving.** You can easily identify that date. Take your calendar, look for the 1st Saturday on that month and then count the 2nd and the THIRD will be the date of your coming together. For example, the third Saturday of the 2020 dates: for October is the 17th; for November is the 21st, for December is the 19th, etc. Those who organize Friday all night prayers for instance, from 12.01 am Third Saturday starts, you can allocate few hours to make decrees. This is why this is a simple strategy that has end-time impact to unite God's people to do what they have always done – PRAY! Let us know if you would join others around the globe until all nations confess that JESUS is indeed LORD. Amen.

NOTE: the Christian Unity Flag can be ordered in two sizes, the small table flags that are 6"x 4" with a stand, and the large flags which are 53" x 48"; these are more like national flags of 'peculiar nations and royals;" Children of God on assignment to unify His Body. All can be ordered through our website: **www.igoafricaforjesus.org.**

Made in the USA
Middletown, DE
21 March 2025